CW01501048

PRAISE FOR THE WILLIAMS BEHAVI

"Bri Williams is the Linnaeus of human behaviour. This is by far the best taxonomy of the different approaches to understanding human behaviour I have ever seen."

Rory Sutherland, Vice Chairman of Ogilvy

"Living up to her name, Bri has written a BRI-lliant guide to behaviour. Here is an easy to follow, highly practical feast of behavioural science that takes us step by step through models to address any problem."

Daniel Ross, host of A Load of BS podcast

"Bri Williams has orchestrated a feast of helpful tools that work to identify and simplify what it takes to change human behaviour – the behaviour of others and, just as critically, our own."

Sam Tatam, Global Principal of Behavioural Science, Ogilvy

"The Behaviour Book cuts to the chase while bringing behavioural science to life. Fun to read and grounded in the realities of modern business, Bri expertly takes us from 'what' to 'how' with relatable and interesting examples. It's a book you and your team will reach for time and again."

Renee Koliba, General Manager at the Austin Group

"Bri so simply yet profoundly articulates how to influence oneself or others to overcome the barriers to behaviour change. This book is a masterclass for salespeople, managers, trainers, therapists, parents, and for oneself where a more desirable behaviour is favoured. Thank you Bri for yet another great book."

Jonathan Senior, Chairman of VeriSmart

"Bri's marvellous book makes behaviour change highly accessible, highly practical and highly enjoyable too. This book will help you solve almost any problem you or your business face. If you never have problems, everyone you meet loves you and everything you touch turns to gold then this is not the book for you. For everyone else, buy this book!"

Chris Rawlinson, Founder of 42 Courses

"Bri Williams' new book does a wonderful job of distilling the best of behavioural science into simple, clear and actionable insights and (best of all) visuals."

Richard Shotton, author of The Choice Factory

"Bri Williams has done it again. The Williams Behaviour Book is the perfect compendium for anyone who wants (or needs) to drive any sort of behavioural change. It doesn't matter whether the change is desired by customers or colleagues, the models in this book, along with the communications strategies outlined, ensure the reader will achieve business or personal improvement. If you can't find a model to change behaviour in this book, then it probably doesn't exist."

Jon Manning, Head of Pricing at MYOB

"This book is a game changer. Bri condenses highly complex psychological insights into digestible and bespoke behaviour models that can be easily accessed, retained and applied in business or personal settings. This is the type of book that you gift to your closest friends, colleagues and clients, knowing that they will undoubtedly find benefits within its pages."

Suzanne Tonks, Managing Director of Oliver and York Public Affairs

THE WILLIAMS BEHAVIOUR BOOK

50 models to influence action

Bri Williams

Author: Bri Williams
Title: The Williams Behaviour Book: 50 models to influence action
Cover design: KiahRani Studios

Your WBBR Code: 25462
Use this code to download png files of the models for free. See page 212 for details.

Disclaimer
All the information, ideas and examples contained in this publication are of a general nature only. Every care has been made to offer ideas about influencing behaviour and it is recommended the reader seek specific advice for their circumstances.

To my parents, Jenny and Keith.

The best models of all.

TABLE OF CONTENTS

INTRODUCTION

PART 2. UNDERSTANDING CUSTOMERS

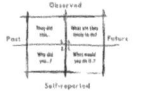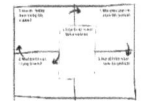
PART 3.TARGETING BY TYPE

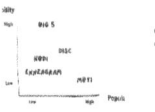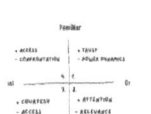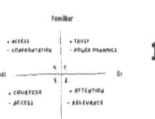

PART 4. IMPROVING COMMUNICATIONS

PART 5. PERSONAL EFFECTIVENESS

What The Williams Behaviour Book is about

This is about:

The science of decision making, distilled into visual models to help you influence behaviour.

Which important because:

Influencing people to take action is rarely easy, and yet success in business relies on being able to do this each and every day.

We want people to respond to our emails, click a button, buy from us, fill out forms correctly, turn up to meetings on time, and so on.

It's not only the behaviour of others that we are trying to influence, of course. Success also relies on influencing *ourselves* to do the better thing. To move more, consume less, start one thing or stop another.

Thankfully, there's a whole world of behavioural science that we can draw on to help influence action more effectively, and that's what The Williams Behaviour Book is about.

It works like this:

The Williams Behaviour Book showcases 50 unique behavioural models that I have developed over the course of my career in applied behavioural science and that I use regularly with my clients. You will not find them anywhere else.

These models will show you how to:
• avoid working on the wrong problem
• convert thoughts into action
• move the unmotivated
• use time more effectively
• give negative feedback

And much more.

Choose your own adventure

Some models are designed to be used in isolation, others in combination. Some cover similar terrain as others, describing different paths or using different analogies to arrive at the same destination. Choose the approach that resonates with you best.

The models are grouped in five sections. You'll find models to:
1. Influence Action – overcome inertia and get people to follow through.
2. Understand Customers – get into your customer's headspace.
3. Target by Type – segment your audience in the right way.
4. Improve Communications – craft the best message, including when to go negative.

5. Improve Personal Effectiveness – use your ancient wiring to manage modern times.

So you never get lost, you'll find the Mega map of all the models and how they relate to one another at the back of this book (page 198).

Language warning

While most models refer to 'customers', you don't need to take that literally. You may find a model equally useful when influencing colleagues, stakeholders, or suppliers. Hey, some models might even be useful at your next family event?

My hope, by sharing the science of influencing action in this visual form, is that you will feel more curious about behaviour, more confident in tackling everyday problems, and more capable in your use of behavioural science.

Let's get influencing!

P.S. Your bonus resources

As a thank you for buying The Williams Behaviour Book, access exclusive and free downloadable versions of the models by:

· Visiting https://www.briwilliams.com/WBBR or

· Scanning the QR code

1. The Simplification Paradox

Why simplicity can be undervalued

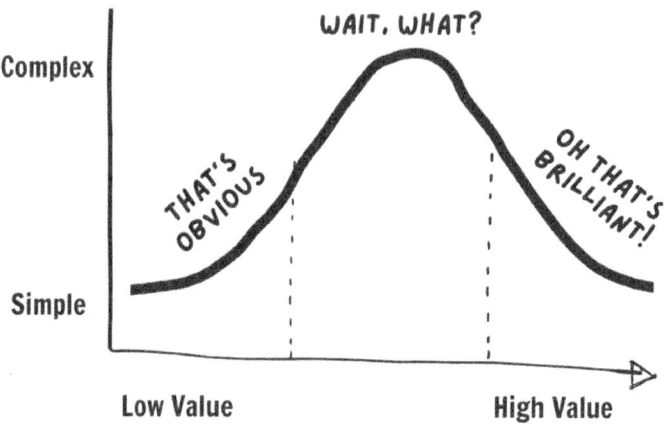

This is about:

Getting people to value something *because* it seems simple.

Which is important because:

In a workplace, colleagues might dismiss your idea. In a consulting role, clients may not want to pay what you believe you are worth. If you're an artist, people might think an 8-year-old could have painted something just as good.

However, in the words of Leonardo da Vinci, 'simplicity is the ultimate sophistication'. Usually things can only seem simple once they have been thoroughly contemplated and refined, and that takes time.

And yet, when convincing others of an idea's merits, its apparent simplicity can mean it is undervalued.

This is the 'Simplification Paradox'. Too simple, people don't value it. Too complex, they won't use it.

It works like this:

When people think an idea (or product or service) is easy to understand, they'll think that's all there is to it. It feels obvious, so anyone could have come up with it.

That can be a problem because complexity is a signifier of value. If it's not complex, it's not valued.

Your task, therefore, is to simplify your idea enough so you engage your customer's interest, but complicate it enough to justify their continued involvement and investment. Once they comprehend its sophistication, your ability to simplify it will be highly valued.

For example:

Take the content of this book. Visual models can — and should — seem simple. Rest assured, there has been a lot of work to get to this point to find, distil and represent lessons from behavioural science in a way that is engaging and useful.

Or let's say you have a solution that you want to table with stakeholders. To avoid it being dismissed as lightweight or too obvious, start the presentation with a brief story of the struggles and complexities you've encountered to get to this point — struggles they themselves are likely to have wrestled with. It is then that you can say, 'which leads me to this moment of clarity...!'

See also:

-> Williams Behaviour Change Model, page 8
-> Creation Vs. Curation, page 192

PART 1.

MODELS FOR INFLUENCING ACTION

How to overcome inertia and get people to act

2. Williams Behaviour Change Model

Anticipating and overcoming barriers to action

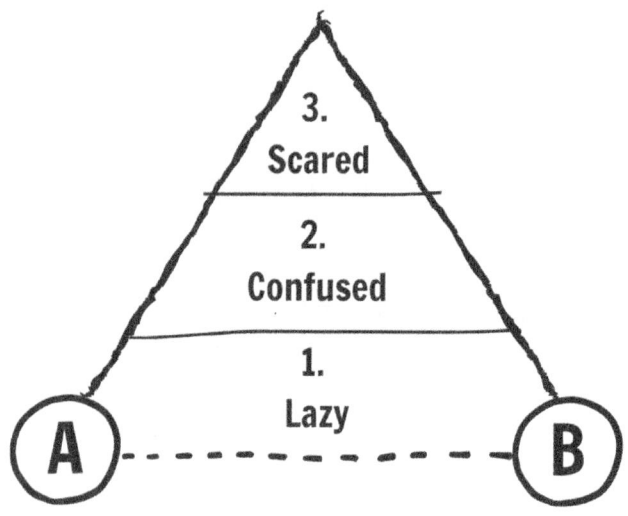

This is about:

Influencing people to take action by anticipating and overcoming three reasons why they won't.

Which is important because:

Everything in business is about getting someone to do something. With customers, that might be staying with you (retention) or switching to you (acquisition). For colleagues, it might be working more, working less, or working differently. For suppliers, it might be prioritising your order over others.

It works like this:

The Williams Behaviour Change Model maps how to identify behavioural barriers.

Your task is to move people from their current behaviour (A) to what you want them to do (B). From not buying to buying, from not clicking to clicking, and from not following a workplace policy to... you get the idea! But how?

Thanks to behavioural and evolutionary science, we know humans are designed to process vast amounts of information very quickly. The downside to this expedience is that it can lead us to rely on habits and associations, frames of reference, rules of thumb and cognitive shortcuts (biases and heuristics).

Boiled down, that means people can be:
• **Lazy**[*] – They are not interested in what you are suggesting. They can't be bothered engaging with, thinking about or acting on your idea, message or product.
• **Confused** – They are interested in what you are suggesting but confused as to what they should do.
• **Scared** – They are interested and know what to do but are worried about proceeding.

*In a cognitive rather than pejorative sense. Formally, this is known as System I processing.

Use the Williams Behaviour Change Model to clarify what behavioural barriers stand in the way of moving your customer from A to B. Some challenges may involve only one of the barriers, others, all three. Revisit the model at different stages of your customer's journey, too. For example, laziness may be a problem early in the purchase process, and fear more of an issue closer to the transaction being finalised.

For example:

You want to influence people under 35 years of age to contribute additional funds to their superannuation. Your behavioural objective is to shift their current behaviour, Not contributing (A), to the desired behaviour, Contributing (B).

To do so you need to address the three barriers to action:

• **Lazy** –They can't see value in doing it now when they won't retire for 30+ years. There's immediate pain but no immediate gain.

• **Confused** –They don't know where to start or how to allocate savings into their superannuation account.

• **Scared** – They are worried about locking away money in superannuation that they can't access until they retire. What if they have unexpected bills or a change in their life circumstances? What if the superannuation fund or regulations change, leaving them short changed?

See also:

-> D-Process for Developing Behavioural Solutions, page 12
-> Behavioural Models Overview, page 16
-> Williams Behaviour Change Venn, page 20
-> Zorro Technique, page 24
-> The Williams Wheel, page 76
-> Meta Model for Influencing Action, page 196

3. D-Process for Developing Behavioural Solutions

Moving from problem to solution

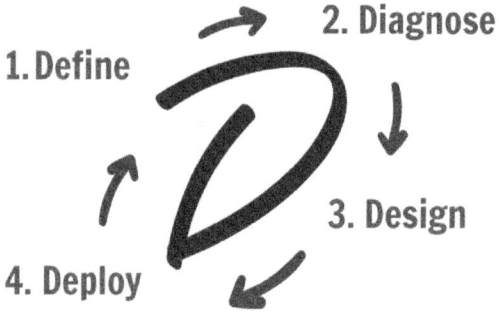

1. Define
2. Diagnose
3. Design
4. Deploy

This is about:

A process to work out what problem you want to solve and how to go about it.

Which is important because:

Problem solving can feel like a knotted ball of Christmas tree lights — a tangle of issues where it's hard to know where to start. D-Process gives you and your colleagues a sense of where you are and where to go next, with the aim to develop effective solutions that are based on the right information and insights.

It works like this:

D-Process for developing behavioural solutions includes four stages:

1. Define

Start by defining your behavioural objective. Who do you want to influence? What do you want them to do? What are they currently doing instead?

2. Diagnose

Now that you know what you want them to do, you need to identify what barriers to action you need to address. To diagnose the situation, you can use the Williams Behaviour Change Model (page 8), along with the Empathy Map (page 108) to get into their headspace and the Customer Insights Landscape (page 80) to identify what you do and do not know about those you wish to influence.

3. Design

Once you know what barriers stand in the way, design your behavioural solution. How are you going to resolve the behavioural challenge? What will your customer experience? Is it a product? A website or App? An email? New language in your copy or a new pricing strategy? Now is the time to draw upon specific biases and heuristics to inform your solution. For example, you might use social norms to engage your customer, help to clarify their decision and overcome their reticence to proceed.

4. Deploy

It's time to deploy the solution and monitor results. Test, iterate, and scale as required, looping back to define your next challenge after successfully achieving your behavioural objective.

For example:

Define

You want website visitors to sign up to your newsletter. Now they are leaving without doing so.

Diagnose

Using the Williams Behaviour Change Model, you realise:

• **Lazy** – There's no obvious benefit to them for signing up.

• **Confused** – There are multiple calls-to-action fighting for their attention on the page.

• **Scared** – You require their date of birth, phone number and surname to sign-up, all of which may seem invasive. They receive no confirmation once they click, so they are not sure whether their action has been a success, which undermines their confidence.

Design

You overhaul the way you invite people to join your newsletter as follows:

• **Lazy** – You lead with the benefit to them by communicating what they get (10% off their order) before what they must give you (their email). Providing a clear, 'what's in it for me?' (WIIFM) heightens their motivation to act.

• **Confused** – You remove competing calls-to-action on the page to make the sign-up more obvious.

• **Scared** – You reduce the sign-up input fields, now only requiring their first name and email. Not only does this reduce effort (overcoming laziness), but it also makes them feel more comfortable to proceed. Once they click, a thank you page appears, confirming their sign-up has worked.

Deploy

You launch a test version of the newsletter sign-up page and compare its conversion with your existing benchmarks. Once you know it is effective, you replace the old page with the improved one. Over the following months you cycle back through D-Process*, experimenting with different rewards, designs, and phrasing to further optimise the customer experience.

---

* My D-Process covers similar stages to models used by other organisations, including BASIC by OECD and DDOTS by Ideas42. Refer to Behavioural Models Overview (page 16) for more.

See also:

-> Williams Behaviour Change Model, page 8

-> Behavioural Models Overview, page 16

-> Williams Change Quadrant, page 58

-> Customer Insights Landscape, page 80

-> Empathy Map, page 108

4. Behavioural Models Overview

Working out what type of behavioural model to use

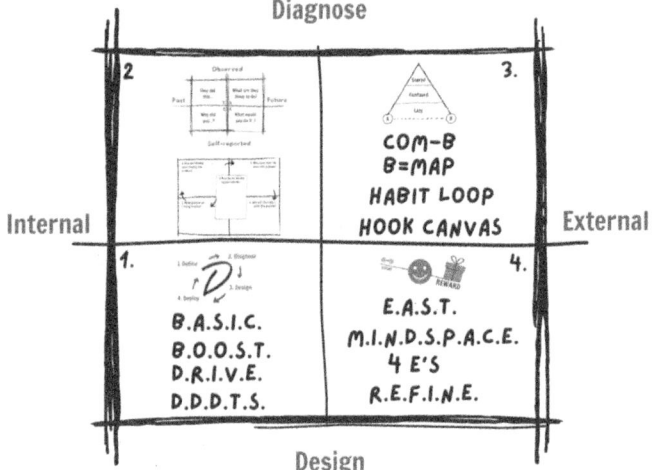

This is about:

Navigating the field of popular behaviour change models so you know which may be most appropriate to use. While not an exhaustive list, I've tried to capture the most commonly used models.

Which is important because:

It's a cluttered landscape with plenty of acronyms to confuse you. It can feel overwhelming. Don't be put off though, because using these models can make a significant difference to your effectiveness.

It works like this:

We can plot a behavioural model along two dimensions: its primary focus and its role in the process.

In terms of **focus**, models tend to be either internally focused (i.e., your organisation) or externally geared (i.e., your customer or market).

In terms of **process**, some models help you diagnose what sort of challenge you have, whereas others help you to design a solution.

1.   Internal-Design

Internal-Design models help you to create a process for your organisation to ultimately design your solution. Most break the process into four or five steps, from inquiry through to implementation.

Examples include:
• **D-Process**: Define-Diagnose-Design-Deploy (Bri Williams, see page 12)
• **BASIC**: Behaviour-Analysis-Strategies-Interventions-Change (OECD)
• **BOOST**: Behaviour-Obstacle-Outline-Study-Tailor (Impactually)
• **DRIVE**: Define-Research-Identify-Validate-Execute (Affective Advisory)
• **DDDTS**: Define-Diagnose-Design-Test-Scale (Ideas42)

2.   Internal-Diagnose

Internal-Diagnose models help you diagnose any gaps in your knowledge about your customers.

Examples include:

• **Customer Insights Landscape**: Identify gaps in your customer insights (Bri Williams, see page 80)

• **Empathy Map:** Shift into the headspace of your customer (Bri Williams, see page 108)

3.   External-Diagnose

External-Diagnose models help you identify fundamental components of behaviour that you will need to draw on to influence your customer. They offer recipes to follow to make behaviour happen.

Examples include:

• **Williams Behaviour Change Model**: Three barriers to behaviour, Lazy, Confused and Scared (Bri Williams, page 8)

• **COM-B**: Behaviour is a function of Capability, Opportunity and Motivation (Michie, van Stralen and West)

• **B-MAP**: Behaviour is a function of Motivation, Ability and being Prompted (Fogg Behaviour Model by BJ Fogg)

• **Hook Canvas**: Trigger-Reward-Action-Investment (Nir Eyal)

• **Habit Loop**: Cue-Routine-Reward (Operant Conditioning Model)

4.   External-Design

External-Design models help you to refine and implement a solution. The danger of jumping straight into these models, is they can seem like a laundry-list of options. For that reason, they should only be applied once you're clear on your behavioural objective. Where External-Diagnose models are like recipes, External-Design models are more like ingredients that you can use to flavour your dish.

Examples include:
• **E Vs. R**: The Effort-Reward equation (Bri Williams, see page 28)
• **EAST**: Easy-Attractive-Social-Timely (UK Behavioural Insights team)
• **MINDSPACE**: Messenger-Incentives-Norms-Defaults-Salience-Priming-Affect-Commitments-Ego (UK Behavioural Insights team)
• **4 E's**: Engage-Enable-Exemplify-Encourage (UK HM Government)
• **REFINE**: Reframe-Facilitate-Incentivise-Encourage (Impactually)

See also:

-> Williams Behaviour Change Model, page 8
-> D-Process for Developing Behavioural Solutions, page 12
-> Effort Vs. Reward Equation, page 28
-> Customer Insights Overview, page 80
-> Empathy Map, page 108

5. Williams Behaviour Change Venn

Relationship between behavioural barriers

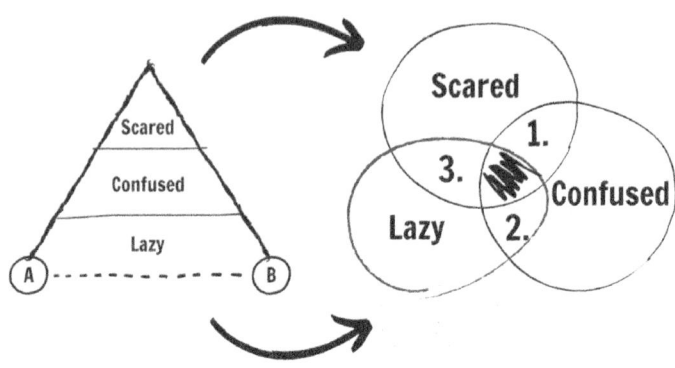

This is about:

Using one behavioural barrier to overcome another.

Which is important because:

You can maximise the impact of behaviour change initiatives by knowing how the barriers to action referred to in the Williams Behaviour Change Model (page 8) interact.

It works like this:

1.   Relationship between Confused and Scared
Customer confusion can stem from bewilderment or a fear of making a poor decision. To feel assured, they either seek more information, which exacerbates overload, or avoid investigating options entirely.

But fear can also sharpen focus. When you present a 'limited edition' option to your customer, for example, it stands out from other choices and clarifies their decision.

2. Relationship between Lazy and Confused

Showcasing a large array of options can attract customer attention and heighten engagement, thereby addressing laziness.

However, as your customer moves towards a final decision, the generous number of options might become confusing.

To reduce the risk of inertia through confusion, and knowing they are lazy thinkers, make it easy for your customer to make a choice. You can use defaults, let them know what the most popular option is, or make a recommendation as a credible authority, for example.

3. Relationship between Scared and Lazy

To renowned writer T. S. Eliot, good poetry makes, 'the familiar strange, and the strange familiar'. The same can be said of influencing people to try new things.

Fear and laziness sit at opposite ends of the response scale. If someone is lazy, they can't be bothered to invest time or effort and are not engaged at all. If they are scared, they are too engaged. They are so psychologically invested that they become scared of committing.

While diametrically opposed, you can use fear to overcome laziness, and laziness to reduce fear.

Make the familiar strange

You can get your customer's attention by making the familiar seem strange, helping them to see something through a fresh perspective. This builds tension about what they may have overlooked or what they'll miss out on if they don't change, motivating them to take action so that dissonant feeling goes away.

Make the strange familiar

You can also use lazy tendencies to overcome fear, making the strange seem familiar. Laziness is about saving cognitive effort by relying on habits and associations. The more you can link the new idea or product with something that is familiar, the more likely they will be to proceed. The Impossible Burger, for example, introduces people to vegan options by simulating the meat they are used to enjoying.

For example:

Overcome a lack of engagement **(laziness)** with:

• **Fear** – When giving a presentation, engage your audience by starting with a provocation, surprise or counterfactual. This 'fear' about what they don't know will heighten engagement.

• **Confusion** – A little bit of chaos can make people more stimulated. Retailer Aldi's special buy bargain bins are an example, where customers enjoy hunting through displays of discounted stock.

Overcome decision paralysis **(confusion)** with:

• **Laziness** – When presenting online shipping options, default your customer to the one you would prefer they use (e.g., Amazon defaults customers to expedited shipping).

• **Fear** – Present options using ticks and crosses to signify what is (or is not) included. Your cheapest option should have the most crosses, making customers anxious about what they'll miss out on if they choose it, thereby increasing the odds that they'll upgrade.

Overcome reticence to commit **(fear)** with:

• **Laziness** – Use metaphor or analogy to make the new seem familiar. The 'Uber of dog minding', for example. The trust and positive sentiment associated with the familiar product will spill over to the new product or idea.

• **Confusion** – When things seem too pristine, customers can worry about doing the wrong thing or making a fool of themselves. People can be scared to enter a shop or restaurant that has no other customers, for example, or be shy to ask a question of a presenter if the audience is quiet. Sometimes making things seem a little messy can help put people at ease. Try some background music to help fill what feels like an empty space and use shop fittings and fixtures to make people feel less exposed and vulnerable.

See also:

-> Williams Behaviour Change Model, page 8
-> Effort Vs. Reward Equation, page 28
-> PES-imistic Paradigm, page 38
-> Behavioural Bowtie, page 42

6. Zorro Technique

Moving the unmotivated

1.BENEFITS of STAYING the same?

2.CONCERNS about STAYING the same?

3. CONCERNS about CHANGE?

4. BENEFITS of CHANGE?

This is about:

Creating desire for change.

Which is important because:

It's easier to get people to change if they've convinced themselves they need to.

It works like this:

You can use the Zorro Technique on your own when planning a change scenario or stakeholder interaction, in conversation with a customer, or when you are leading a team of colleagues through a change program.

Run through four questions in the following sequence:

1. **What are the benefits of staying the same?**
This lets people express what's good about how things currently are, and recognise they already do many things well.

2. **What concerns do you have about staying as we are?**
People always have niggles about how things are currently done, so this question invites them to put them on the table. Doing so creates tension about sticking with the status quo and opens the door to considering what could be done differently.

3. **If we change, what concerns do you have?**
It's normal to have concerns about the unknown, so this allows people to share their reservations. It also means you (and they) can develop mitigations.

4. **What are the benefits of changing?**
End on a positive by asking what the benefits of trying things differently will be. This helps people envisage the new world and want to work towards it.

For example:

You want your communications team to apply behavioural science to their work, but past efforts to convince them have failed.

You gather the team in a workspace (physical or virtual), and lead them through the questions.

1.   **Benefits of staying the same** – We know what we're doing; we can turn communications around quickly; we don't have time to learn new things.

2.   **Concerns about staying the same** – Our communications are not getting the traction we need them to; stakeholders are bombarding us with requests for more communications and we can't say no.

3.   **Concerns about changing** – What if these new techniques don't work? What if I feel stupid or get it wrong?

4.   **Benefits of changing** – We get better cut-through; we influence stakeholders to brief us earlier and more precisely; we strengthen perceptions of our work and how it contributes to the business; we develop new skills; looks good on the resume!

See also:

-> Williams Behaviour Change Model, page 8
-> Behavioural Bowtie, page 42
-> Conversational Cutlery, page 54

7. Effort Vs. Reward Equation

Making behaviour happen

1. REWARD EFFORT ✗
2. EFFORT REWARD ✗
3. EFFORT REWARD ✓

This is about:

The relationship between rewards for doing something and the effort involved.

Which is important because:

Rewards do not always motivate action. We often talk to customers about the benefits of doing what we would like them to do but forget that there's another side to the behavioural equation: effort.

It works like this:

When contemplating whether to do something, people weigh up two sides of an equation: effort and reward.

Effort includes time and financial cost as well as emotional and physiological outlays. Things like how many times your website visitor must swipe or click, how long they are left on hold when they call, and how many fields they have to complete on a form.

Reward is their payoff. This can likewise be financial or time related (Save money! Save time!) but may also include psychological benefits like status or certainty.

If you want behaviour to happen, the simple rule is rewards for proceeding must exceed effort. Let's look at why.

1.   Effort exceeds Reward (E > R)
If effort is greater than reward, behaviour won't happen. This sounds obvious once it's pointed out, but you may be overlooking the effort you're asking of customers and therefore underweighting the associated reward. Remember, to proceed with what you're suggesting, customers have to give something up or change what they're used to, and that takes effort.

2.   Effort equals Reward (E = R)
Behaviour won't happen if effort is equal to reward, either. Why bother expending effort just to receive benefits that are commensurate with what they have?

3.   Reward exceeds Effort (R > E)

For behaviour to happen, reward must be greater than effort. In fact, the payoff has to be roughly *double* the effort of changing to displace the status quo.

For example:

Let's say a bank is trying to lure a customer away from the incumbent by offering savings of 0.25% on their home loan. What might stop the customer from jumping on the deal? Effort. To switch banks means phone calls, paperwork, and changing their direct debits. Can they really be bothered right now?

To get them to act, the bank needs to make the reward more obvious, such as expressing the saving in real terms (e.g., if your current loan is $x, you will save $y) rather than an abstract (and seemingly small) percentage. They also need to reduce real and perceived effort as much as possible (e.g., switching is easy because we look after x, all you need to do is y).

Or perhaps you are pitching to become a client's new software supplier? While the reward for them is clear — you can save them money and time — you are concerned that they may think it is too difficult to change.

As part of your pitch, you therefore outline how switching is easy, including the dedicated customer support you offer, the paperwork you'll take care of (you'll even manage the

---

relationship with the old supplier!), and the minimal downtime they'll experience because you'll complete the transfer in non-work hours.

See also:

-> Williams Behaviour Change Model, page 8
-> Behavioural Bowtie, page 42
-> Creation Vs. Curation, page 192

Porter Principle

Carrying your customer's bags

This is about:

Carrying your customer's bags, metaphorically.

Which is important because:

Customers don't want more to do. Take weight off their shoulders, don't add to it.

It works like this:

1.   Make it as easy as possible for your customer to work with you. Take care of paperwork, reduce decision points, provide progess updates and summaries of longer documents, minimise friction in your processes and anticipate their needs.

2.   Take the opportunity in your communications to remind them (subtly) that you are committed to making their life easier. Phrases like, 'let me', 'I'll take care of', and 'leave that to me' will help them to feel looked after.

For example:

Imagine that you are sending your customer an invoice for payment. Instead of, 'here's your invoice', which sounds like a burden for them, rephrase it as 'I've arranged an invoice for you', so it sounds like you've done something on their behalf.

Diary scheduling is one of the biggest burdens, so rather than asking them to 'let me know when is convenient', (which places the responsibility on them), use a calendar scheduling tool (e.g., Calendly) that lets them find a time that suits them, or list a few options in your email that they can easily choose from.

See also:

-> Williams Behaviour Change Model, page 8
-> Effort Vs. Reward Equation, page 28
-> Empathy Map, page 108

9. Timing Rewards

Maximising the impact of employee rewards

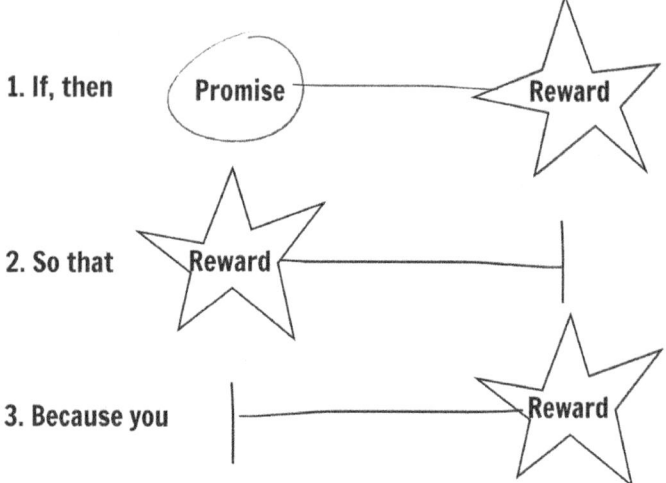

1. If, then   Promise — Reward

2. So that   Reward

3. Because you   Reward

This is about:

Timing employee rewards to have the maximum impact on performance.

Which is important because:

It's not just whether you reward employees, but when.

It works like this:

Let's look at three options for rewarding employees:

1.   'If/Then' rewards

'If/then' rewards are promised upfront and delivered once your employee has achieved what they needed to. The reward is contingent on their performance. You pay staff a $2,000 bonus if they meet year-end financial goals, for example.

While this is a common reward mechanism, that doesn't mean it is most effective because the payoff can seem too distant or abstract to motivate day-to-day behaviour.

2.   'So that' rewards

'So that' rewards are another form of contingent reward, but they are paid upfront to encourage performance. Also known as 'clawback' rewards, the employee has to repay the reward if they fail to achieve what's required. You pay staff a $2,000 bonus at the start of the year, for example, which they have to pay back if they do not meet year-end financial goals.

Paying something back is more psychologically painful than missing out on a reward that's promised (an if/then scenario) because people are loss averse. In other words, we try harder because we are worried about losing money we have already pocketed.

The significant risk with 'so that' rewards, is your employee resenting you for making them pay money back. Not great for team morale!

3.   'Because you' rewards

An underutilised and highly effective approach to rewarding performance is 'because you', where you reward them unexpectedly. For example, you give one of your team members a $200 voucher to a fancy restaurant because they went above and beyond for a client presentation last week.

This spontaneous recognition of great work engenders a spirit of reciprocity, where your staff will want to return your act of kindness with enhanced performance. It also capitalises on intrinsic rather than extrinsic rewards. In other words, people work harder because it makes them feel good rather than because they are paid.

Timing is key with 'because you' rewards. You want to provide them close to when the behaviour occurs, encouraging more of it.

To offset any risk that you are seen to favour some staff over others, be sure others know why the behaviour is being recognised.

See also:

-> Effort Vs. Reward Equation, page 28
-> Momentum Model, page 158
-> Forget the Shit Sandwich, page 166

10. PES-imistic Paradigm

What customers really fear

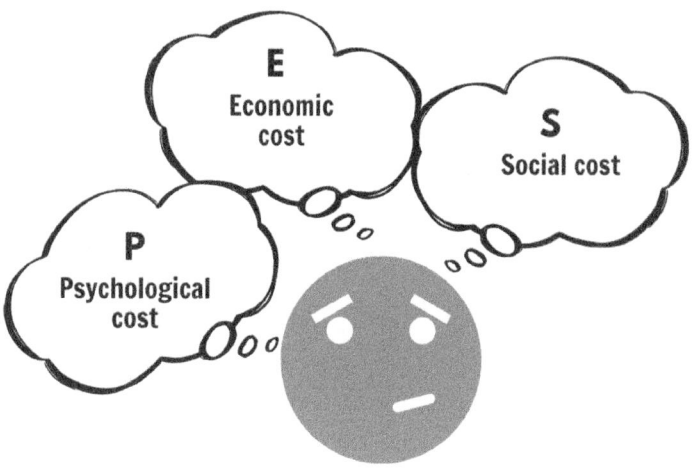

This is about:

Three types of fears your customer may have.

Which is important because:

Your customer may choose not to proceed for a reason they haven't shared with you. For instance, they might cite price as an objection, but really, it's their fear of making the wrong choice that's the problem.

It works like this:

Fears fall into three buckets: psychological, economic and social (PES):

• **P**sychological – Anxiety due to the uncertainty of the process or outcome, or of having more work to do.

• **E**conomic – Money and/or time they'll lose if this goes wrong, or the extra cost if things go well.

• **S**ocial – Threats to their credibility and/or status. Will this cause them embarrassment? Will people resent their success?

For example:

	Fear of it going wrong	Fear of it going right
P **Psychological concerns**	Fear of being punished for the decision; fear of being wrong.	Fear of the new - moving away from the comfort of the status quo; stress of extra work they'll have to take on.
E **Economic concerns**	Money or time they'll waste.	Being able to afford it; extra staffing they'll require.
S **Social concerns**	Damage to their credibility/status for making the decision; fear of being wrong or disliked.	Having to convince others this is a good idea; having to lead people through change; tall poppy syndrome.

List the fears you imagine your customers may have:

	P Psychological concerns	E Economic concerns	S Social concerns
Fear of it going wrong			
Fear of it going right			

See also:

-> Williams Behaviour Change Model, page 8
-> Empathy Map, page 108
-> Frame the Gain Vs. Loss is Boss, page 154
-> Forget the Shit Sandwich, page 166
-> Certainty Matrix, page 168

11. Behavioural Bowtie

The sweet spot between fear and loafing

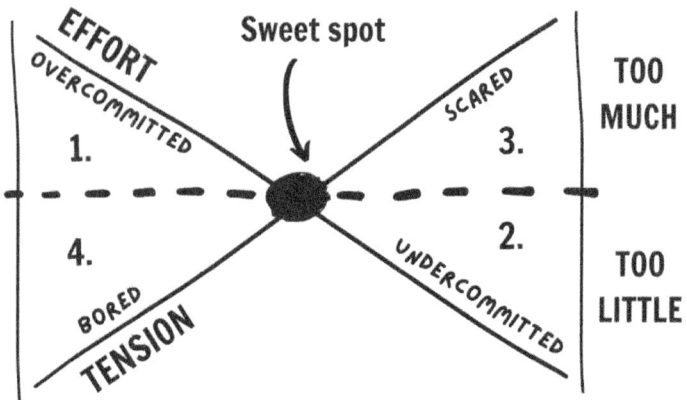

This is about:

The sweet spot between asking too much or too little of customers.

Which is important because:

When convincing someone to do something, sometimes it's hard to know if you've pushed too hard or not hard enough.

It works like this:

There are two things to get right when influencing action — effort and tension. How much you make your customer do and how much you make them feel.

Too much or too little tension or effort, and they won't do what you want.

1.   Too much effort - Your customer will avoid what you're asking because it's too difficult or resource depleting. They feel overcommitted.

2.   Too little effort - They'll avoid it because they don't feel involved. They feel under committed.

3.   Too much tension - Your customer will avoid what you're asking of them because they are scared of proceeding.

4.   Too little tension - They won't bother engaging because they are bored.

The sweet spot is when they feel personally involved (they have 'skin in the game'), and are motivated to proceed.

For example:

Customers ignore your email requesting they provide personal information.

Things to look at:

1.   Too much effort – Do they have to download a form? Print their answers? Scan and return it to you? Is the form blank and they have to provide answers that you should already know (e.g., their name, email, address and customer reference number)?

2.   Too little effort – Have you forgotten to ask them to do something, or is the Call-to-Action unclear so they don't think they need to respond?

3.   **Too much tension** – Do you seem credible? Have you proved who you are? Have you explained why and how you'll use the information? Does your link look like spam?

4.   **Too little tension** – Have you explained what happens if they don't take action? What might they miss out on? Have you created a sense of urgency or importance?

See also:

-> Williams Behaviour Change Model, page 8

-> PES-imistic Paradigm, page 38

-> Conversational Cutlery, page 54

-> Frame the Gain Vs. Loss is Boss, page 154

12. Lily Pad Leaping Lesson

Getting customers take the leap

This is about:

Influencing your customer to move from their existing situation, position or behaviour to a new one.

Which is important because:

We spend most of our time and energy influencing ourselves or others to change in some way, yet our efforts are too often ineffective. Why? It's often easier for people to stick with what they have.

It works like this:

Imagine you are trying to get your customer (the frog) to leave their current lily pad (A) and move to the new lily pad (B). There are three approaches to use, and while they can be used separately, they are most powerful in combination.

1.   Entice with benefits

The most common approach is to entice your frog with the promise of how great lily pad B is. For example, it might save them money or time.

'Sounds great!', your frog thinks, and they decide to take the leap.

There's a real chance this enthusiasm might recede, however. We see this commonly with health behaviours, where people want to make changes but their initial motivation falls away. While there's a benefit in the longer-term for exercising or eating differently, that's not enough to get them acting in the right way, right now.

That's because motivation is not stable — it ebbs and flows. Some days you have it, some days you don't. That means it can't be relied upon to sustain behavioural change.

To make sure our frog completes the change journey, you have to bolster their enthusiasm along the way with benefits they can enjoy immediately, not just once they've reached B.

For example:
The Noom health app keeps people moving towards their longer term goals by reinforcing positive behaviours as they progress. Users get praise from the Noom community and coaches, and the satisfaction of seeing a graph of their results move in a positive direction.

2.   Make the current state unpalatable

A.

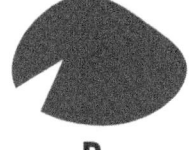

B.

Frogs can get very comfortable with their existing lily pad. This is the status quo — our innate preference to leave things as they are. As good as lily pad B might be, the security and familiarity of lily pad A holds sway.

Your task is therefore to make lily pad A seem unattractive, shining a light on the downside of sticking with the 'old' lily pad. Is it outdated? Is it at risk of sinking? Might it leave them stranded and isolated from all the other frogs?

Making A seem unpalatable will increase your customer's appetite to try something new.

For example:
Let's say you give customers a free trial version of your software. To motivate them to upgrade to the paid version, you reveal features that they can't access through the free plan.

Or imagine you are an airline. You deliberately make passengers in Economy class walk through Business to see how much more room they could enjoy. Then, to heighten aspirational exclusivity, you pull the curtain across to separate the haves and have nots!

3.   Make it easy to change

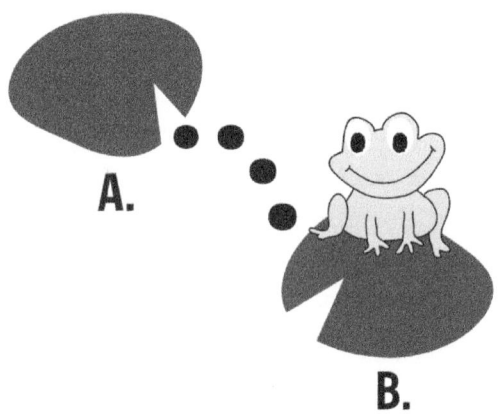

A.

B.

While approaches 1 and 2 can be effective, they rely on the frog's motivational state. As we know, motivation is fleeting and you can waste a lot of time and money getting your customers or employees enthused, only for that to drop away the next day.

Instead, to get your frog to jump from A to B, the most effective approach is to minimise effort required. The easier something is, the less motivated they need to be.

The question to ask yourself then, is how can we make moving to lily pad B seem simple?

For example:
You are a utilities provider who takes care of all the paperwork required to switch your new customer from their old provider.

See also:

-> Effort Vs. Reward Equation, page 28
-> The Porter Principle, page 32
-> Move Away Vs. Move Towards, page 52
-> Fuzzy Future Self, page 96

13. Move Away Vs. Move Towards

Moving forward means letting go

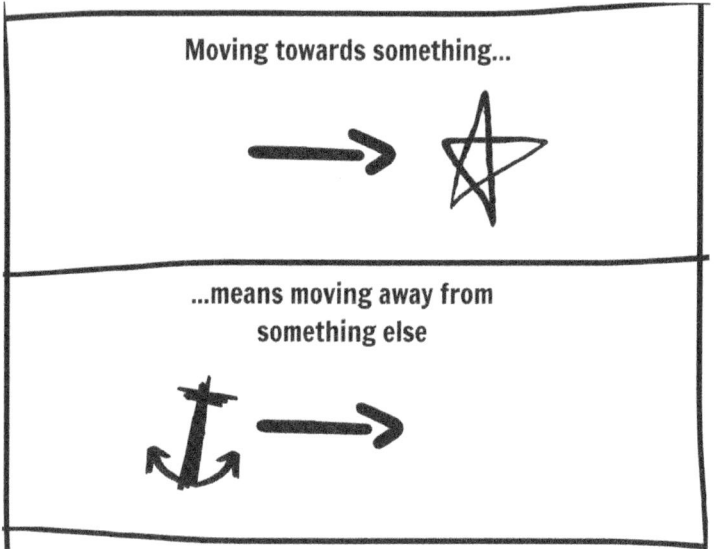

Moving towards something...

...means moving away from something else

This is about:

Remembering that for customers to move towards something, they have to move away from something else.

Which is important because:

We get excited about what people gain from working with or buying from us and overlook what they have to give up. Selling benefits is only one dimension of your task.

It works like this:

To get people to proceed, they need to be weaned off the current status quo.

For example:

Moving to a new bank means moving away from your current one, and that means new card numbers and PINs, setting up new direct debits and changing all existing payment arrangements. The new bank must make this worthwhile for you to bother!

See also:

-> Effort Vs. Reward Equation, page 28
-> The Lily Pad Leaping Lesson, page 46
-> Williams Change Quadrant, page 58

14. Conversational Cutlery

Closing the sale

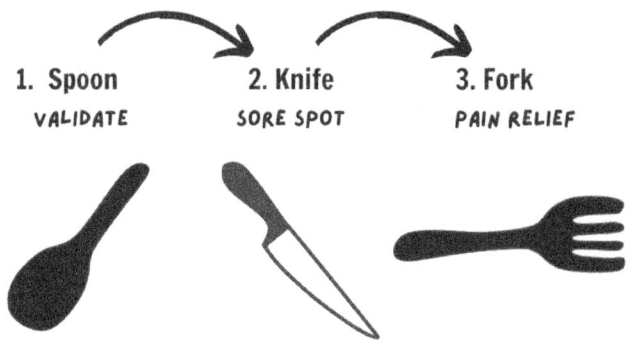

1. **Spoon**
VALIDATE

2. **Knife**
SORE SPOT

3. **Fork**
PAIN RELIEF

This is about:

Securing a commitment to buy in your sales conversation.

Which is important because:

Sometimes we have great conversations with our customers but they don't result in a sale, which can be a waste of time for both parties.

It works like this:

There are three parts to an effective sales conversation: The spoon, and knife and the fork.

Part 1. The spoon: Validation and relaxation

The first thing we need to do in a sales conversation is to prove we are on our customer's wave length. We do this by listening and validating their situation.

We want to normalise their frustrations and experiences so they relax and feel understood. Most people will be defensive in a sales meeting. They will be on guard and nervous about being pressured into buying. This stage is therefore about diffusing that tension and helping them feel that they are in control.

Use prompts like, 'tell me more about that?' and supportive statements like 'yes, that must be really difficult to manage'.

Why the 'spoon', though? Two reasons. First, just like we can use a spoon as a mirror, we want to reflect what they share back to them. And second, a spoon is a bit like the shape of an ear, reminding us to listen.

Once we've done that — once we've shown a sincere interest, it's time to delve a little deeper. It's time for the knife.

Part 2. The knife: Cutting to the core issue

The second stage in a sales conversation is to cut through and explore with them why they are in this situation.

Where part 1 is about neutralising tension about being sold something they don't want, in part 2 we start to create tension by examining the cause of their issue. This is cutting through the context to reveal the true pain point — the sore spot that keeps them up at night.

Language like 'what I've observed across your industry (normalising their pain) is that x is increasingly becoming a problem. Is that the same for you?'

The aim of this stage is to have them reveal and acknowledge they have a problem. That gives you license to share how you have helped people in similar situations, and what it might look like for them.

Part 3. The fork: Defining the path forward

The fork is the 'fork in the road', where we draw everything we've talked about together to a decision point. We put the decision to them by contrasting one option (not buying) with another (buying).

This is powerful because it clarifies the situation for them. It reminds them that the status quo — their choice to do nothing about the issue, is still a choice, and that choice carries a downside. By contrasting the two future paths, we make not proceeding seem unpalatable, while making our offer to take the pain away seem attractive.

Does the fork in the road have to be only two options? No, you can use three, but any more than that becomes unwieldy.

For example:

Closing with two options

'As I see it, you have two options. The first is you continue on the path you're on. It might be okay for a while, but from what you've shared with me, that comes with some major downsides.

Or...we can take care of it. If you work with me, that would mean we do x so you can y. With those two options in mind, what would you like to do?'

Closing with three options

'From what you've shared I see three options for you. The first is to do nothing about this, and that means you're likely to continue to see the same results. From what you've told me this isn't acceptable.

The second is to invest in a full scale review of operations, in which case we're looking at probably 6 months and close to $100,000. In my opinion this is probably more than is required.

Or the third is to start with a pilot program, where we start with two stores and can be up and running within 6 weeks. With those options in mind, what would you like to do?'

See also:

-> Move Away Vs. Move Towards, page 52
-> Choosing Choices, page 72

15. Williams Change Quadrant

Four levels of change

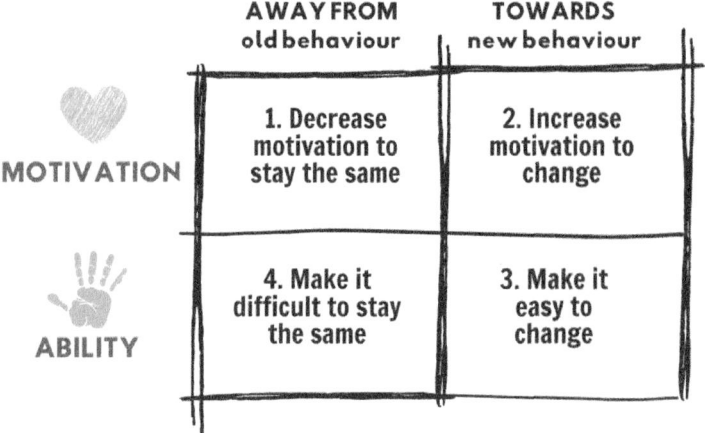

This is about:

Four ways to encourage behaviour change.

Which is important because:

Sometimes we don't know where to start, or our attempts to encourage change fall flat because we've used only one method when we should have combined it with others.

It works like this:

The Williams Change Quadrant breaks behaviour change down into four dimensions:

- **Motivation** – How your customer feels
- **Ability** – Your customer's ability to act
- **Moving away from** – Leaving something behind
- **Moving towards** – Gaining something new.

Motivation is an emotional state, and you can use these desires to move people towards the new behaviour or away from the old.

That means decreasing their motivation to stay the same (1) or increasing motivation to change (2). While these might seem the same, they carry different psychological weight. For example, the motivation to move away from something deemed unpleasant (like a bad smell or late fee) can be much stronger than moving towards something pleasant (like a nice smell or discount).

For example:

Your goal is to get healthier.

1. **Decrease motivation to stay the same** – Make old eating or movement behaviours undesirable, emphasising what to stop doing. Watching a documentary on the effects of sugar might turn you off ice cream, for example.
2. **Increase motivation to change** – Make fitness behaviours desirable, moving towards new health behaviours. Your focus here will be on rewarding what you want to start doing, like going to the gym or eating more vegetables.

While motivation can spark behaviour change, it tends to be as unstable and fleeting as a New Year's resolution — some days your customer will have it and some days they won't.

That's why you are better off focusing on your customer's **ability** to change.

You can make the change easy to accomplish (3) by eliminating friction, or you can make it difficult to continue the old behaviour (4) by adding friction.

3.   **Make it easy to change** – Pre-cutting vegetables so they are easy to cook with, or keeping fruit on the kitchen counter to make healthy snacking more likely.

4.   **Make it difficult to stay the same** – Storing indulgent snacks out of sight, installing a lock on the pantry door, removing the office chair so you have to use your standing desk.

See also:

-> Williams Behaviour Change Model, page 8
-> Effort Vs. Reward Equation, page 28
-> The Lily Pad Leaping Lesson, page 46
-> Move Away Vs. Move Towards, page 52
-> Customer Retention Strategies, page 62

16. Customer Retention Strategies

How to keep your customers

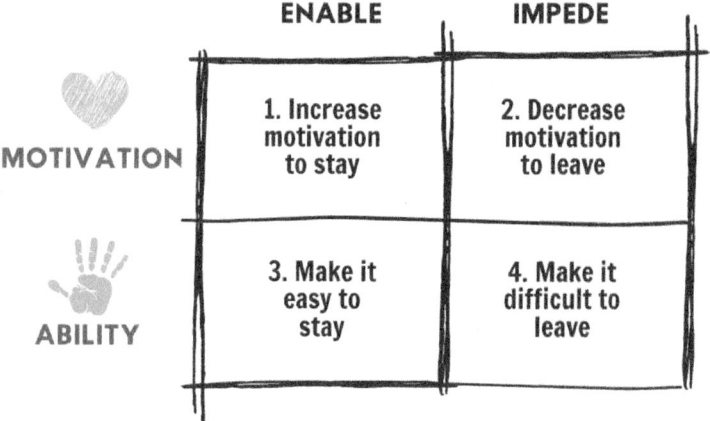

	ENABLE	**IMPEDE**
MOTIVATION	1. Increase motivation to stay	2. Decrease motivation to leave
ABILITY	3. Make it easy to stay	4. Make it difficult to leave

This is about:

Four ways to keep your customers.

Which is important because:

You worked hard to get your customers and retaining them is usually the most cost effective thing you can do.

It works like this:

Keeping customers boils down to how your customers feel about you (their motivation to stay or leave), and/or how easy they find it to stay with you (their ability to undertake the action).

In terms of **motivation**, you can:

1.   **Increase motivation to stay** – they feel good about staying because they receive benefits for doing so (like excellent customer service or preferential pricing) and/or

2.   **Decrease motivation to leave** – they feel worried about leaving because of what they'll risk losing (like the security of knowing what they can expect or years of membership benefits).

While these two seem the same, they work on different psychological levers. Wanting to stay is an affirmative, positive sentiment. Not wanting to leave is a fear-framed choice, where they instead seek to avoid a negative outcome.

In terms of **ability**, you can:

3.   **Make it easy to stay** – the renewal process is effortless; or

4.   **Make it difficult to leave** – the cancellation process is difficult.

For example:

1.   **Increase motivation to stay** – treat them well throughout their relationship with you and/or offer a discount for staying.

2.   **Decrease motivation to leave** – give them 'loyalty' points the longer they stay with you. If they leave, they lose the points and have to start all over again, making it a painful choice.

3.   **Make it easy to stay** – offer auto-renewal or make the renewal process as easy as possible (e.g., click from email straight to payment page).

4.   **Make it difficult to leave** – add friction to the
cancellation process (e.g., they have to call you rather than do it
online). Making it difficult to leave is not recommended because
you'll soon get a reputation for treating customers poorly, which
will stifle your ability to attract new customers and staff.

See also:

-> Williams Behaviour Change Model, page 8
-> Effort Vs. Reward Equation, page 28
-> PES-imistic Paradigm, page 38
-> Behavioural Bowtie, page 42
-> Williams Change Quadrant, page 58
-> Frame the Gain Vs. Loss is Boss, page 154

17. Partitioning Principle

How to help people stop

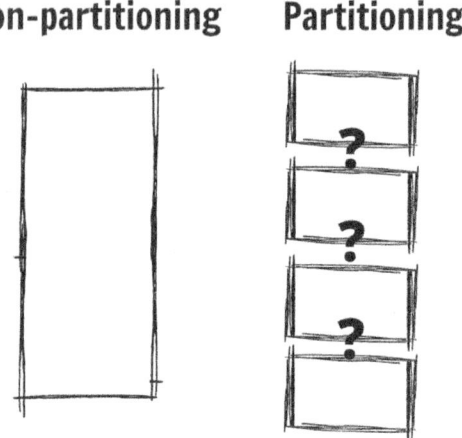

This is about:

The value of being able to stop.

Which is important because:

Sometimes we continue with a behaviour even when we shouldn't. We might eat a whole packet of chips or binge a series on Netflix simply because it's easier to continue than it is to stop.

Many businesses prey on this, of course, and want their customers to endlessly (and mindlessly) consume their product.

But some customers want help in managing their self-control, and willingly pay a premium for it. This is called 'partitioning', where smaller, discrete units are sought out by customers to help them monitor and control their consumption. Single serve chocolates are an example.

It works like this:

Adding breaks — or partitions — into a product or experience can help the user exert more control over their consumption. Effectively, they are confronted by more frequent 'go/no go' decision points, interrupting their otherwise mindless consumption. Your customer values this friction because it helps them moderate their behaviour.

For example:

Many streaming services auto-play the next episode to encourage their customers to keep watching. Some now cap the number of episodes that are automatically served, forcing the viewer to make a decision whether to continue.

See also:

-> Effort Vs. Reward Equation, page 28
-> Moderators Vs. Eliminators, page 186
-> Three C's of Habit Ease, page 188

18. Decision-Action Conversion

Ensuring customers follow through

This is about:

The gap between your customer making a decision and acting on it.

Which is important because:

The job isn't complete once a decision is made — that decision needs to result in an action, otherwise it is just a thought. A customer deciding to buy, for example, means nothing unless they actually go through with the transaction.

It works like this:

When making sure a decision turns into an action, you have two dimensions to consider.

The first is **temporal proximity** — in other words, how quickly the action follows the decision.

The greater the time between the decision and action, the greater the likelihood the action won't happen. There's more risk of interference, distraction and second-guessing. Intensity drops, and motivation with it. A customer might get excited about a product, decide to sleep on it, and lose interest the following day.

We can describe the gap between a decision and action as either

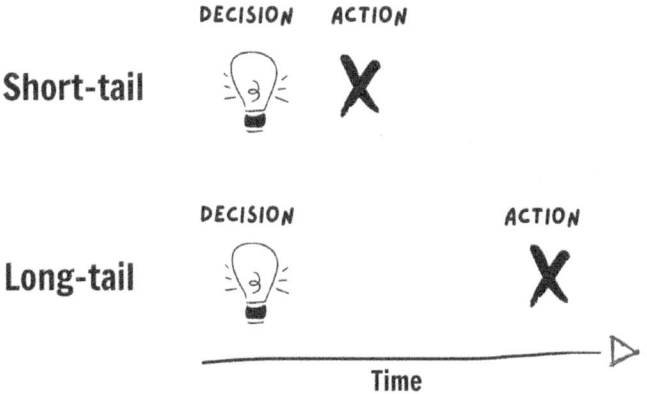

Short-tail, where hardly any time passes at all, or **Long-tail**, when there is a longer gap.

Deciding to eat a snack is typically short-tail, for example, whereas deciding to change jobs is long-tail.

The second dimension is the degree of '**boundedness**' — in other words, how committed your customer is, either psychologically or systemically, to follow through. How easy is it to get out of the action? What's their accountability to themselves and others?

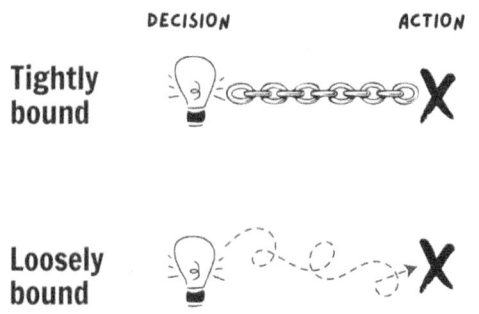

Tightly bound means it's difficult for your customer to back out. Making the decision is as good as acting on it because there are guardrails — systems, processes, or pressures — that funnel them towards the action.

A judge's decision, for example, is tightly bound because once made, the legal system kicks in and the decision is enacted as a matter of course. Likewise in real estate, where buyers sign a contract and pay a deposit. Yes, they can extricate themselves, but it comes with a cost.

Loosely bound means they can back out easily. The decision is more malleable; a suggestion rather than mandate; an idea rather than commitment.

Many consumer decisions are loosely bound. As abandonme. rates attest, adding to an online shopping cart is no guarantee that your customer will go through with the purchase.

To maximise Decision-Action Conversion, you can shorten the time between decision and action, and increase the degree of boundedness.

For example:

Shorten the tail

- Use 'early bird' discounts to gain commitment sooner.
- Provide reassurances like a money back guarantee or cooling off period to allay concerns about committing to you.
- Reduce stock availability or promote an imminent price rise to create urgency.

Increase boundedness

- Require customers to sign a contract if you are selling professional services.
- Invoice customers immediately for a deposit.
- Get them using the product immediately so they feel psychological ownership.

See also:

-> Effort Vs. Reward Equation, page 28
-> Fuzzy Future Self, page 96

ng Choices

How many options to present

1. Yes or no?

2. This or that?

3. Which?

This is about:

How many options to present to your customer.

Which is important because:

With too few options, you risk not attracting any customers. With too many, you may overwhelm them.

Furthermore, if you stock physical goods, the greater the number of options you have, the more expensive and complex your inventory management becomes.

It works like this:

How many options to present will ultimately be a function of your business structure and competitive context. Here are some pros and cons to consider:

One option

The clear advantage of a single option is simplicity. Your customer is clear on what it is you are offering. Do you want a black t-shirt or not?

But single options can trigger 'Single Option Aversion', which is when customers react badly to the lack of choice and feel they need to keep searching for alternatives. To avoid this, give them context to reassure them that you are one of a kind for a reason.

For example:

'You won't find another black t-shirt like this. While to the untrained eye some t-shirts look similar, ours respond to your individual body chemistry using patented materials and technology.'

Two options

Use two options when you want a 'this or that' decision. For example, do you want the t-shirt in black or white? Where a single option narrows the decision path to yes or no, offering a choice of two options shifts your customer from a 'will I or won't I?' decision to a 'which one?' frame of mind.

A word of caution, though. When two options are presented,

customers can get stuck trying to work out which they prefer. If there is no clear winner, the torture of having to choose between equally good options can make them walk away from both.

For that reason, have ways to break the deadlock or make buying both a reasonable path.

For example:
'The t-shirt comes in black and white. We find black is the most popular,' or 'buy one, get the second ½ price'.

Three options
Expanding options to three is best when you want people to feel they have an array of choices. It also avoids the deadlock 'this or that' of two options, because a third option tends to direct attention to the middle. If you can't decide between the black and white t-shirts, perhaps grey is the perfect compromise?

Known as the 'Goldilocks effect' or "Extremeness aversion', your customer will typically avoid choices at the extreme of a choice array and settle for the safety of the middle instead.

For that reason, be sure that your middle option has the highest margin and is something you want to sell!

For example:
'The black t-shirt is $99, the grey is $78, and the white is $69.'

See also:

-> Williams Behaviour Change Model, page 8
-> Williams Behaviour Change Venn, page 20

20. The Williams Wheel

How to perpetuate behaviour change

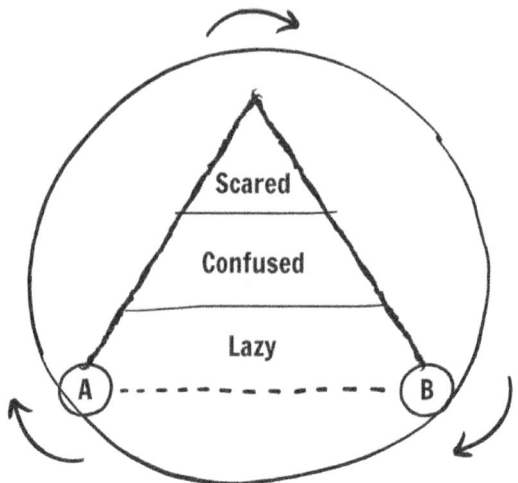

This is about:

Behaviour change being an ongoing cycle rather than one-off event.

Which is important because:

Behavioural impact doesn't stop once your customer or colleague has moved from their current behaviour (A) to the desired behaviour (B).

Instead, B becomes the current status quo (A) and the cycle continues. What do you want your customer to do next?

It works like this:

As the original desired behaviour is now the current, status quo behaviour, you start the process afresh by defining your new behavioural objective, i.e., what's the new B? From there you work through the three barriers of the Williams Behaviour Change Model (Lazy, Confused and Scared, page 8) that stand in the way of success.

For example:

You successfully moved a customer from your competitor (A) to you (B) by selling them your entry-level package. Your next task is to upsell them from the basic package (A) to the premium version (B).

See also:

-> Williams Behaviour Change Model, page 8
-> D-Process for Developing Behavioural Solutions, page 12
-> Behavioural Models Overview, page 16

PART 2.

MODELS FOR UNDERSTANDING CUSTOMERS

How your customers are wired to see their world

21. Customer Insights Landscape

Identifying gaps in what you know about your customers

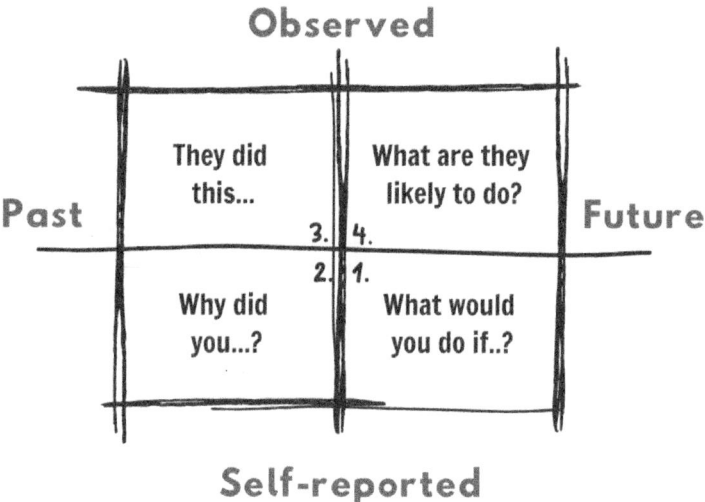

This is about:

Identifying gaps in what you know about your customers by mapping the information you have or can gain.

Which is important because:

This is the best way to get a full picture of their behaviour. Otherwise, you might have a distorted view, leading you to overinvest time, money or trust in some sources of information while underinvesting in others.

It works like this:

You can analyse behaviour in two ways: you can ask people and you can observe what they do.

Asking them produces **self-reported** behaviour, where they share what they plan to do or explain why they did something. Most commonly, this type of information is gathered through focus groups, customer interviews, and satisfaction surveys.

You can ask them **future-oriented** questions like, 'what would you do or feel if ...?' (quadrant 1), or you can ask **past-oriented** questions like, 'why did you choose...', or 'what did you feel when...?' (quadrant 2).

As compelling as self-reported behaviour may seem, it is subject to storytelling and sensemaking. This means what they say doesn't necessarily translate to real behaviour. Customers might tell you that they'll buy your product if it has a particular feature, but they don't.

Observed behaviour is watching to see what customers do or have done rather than asking them. (Not as creepy as it sounds, I promise!)

Past-oriented observed behaviour is proof of what they actually did — sales receipts or website visits, for example (quadrant 3). While accurate, the challenge is turning past behaviour into future behaviour, because that's what you are probably most interested in. You want to know: if we do x, what will they do in response?

Which brings us to customer insights nirvana: future-oriented, observed behaviour (quadrant 4).

While it's the most difficult to get, it is possible. How? By using behavioural research based on field experiments, which observe rather than ask about behaviour. From such research we can extract decision making patterns (biases and heuristics), that help us understand how humans are wired and use these principles to predict future behaviour.

For example:

Imagine that you're an Australian producer of tinned fruit and vegetables. You run customer focus groups and interviews, and people tell you that they support buying Australian produce (1).

However, sales data from the supermarket tells a different story, with people buying the imported Italian tomatoes instead (3).

Seeking to understand, you commission market researchers to interview shoppers who tell you that they prefer the taste of the Italian produce (2). They don't mention price, even though you know this pattern emerges when the Italian tomatoes are on sale (3).

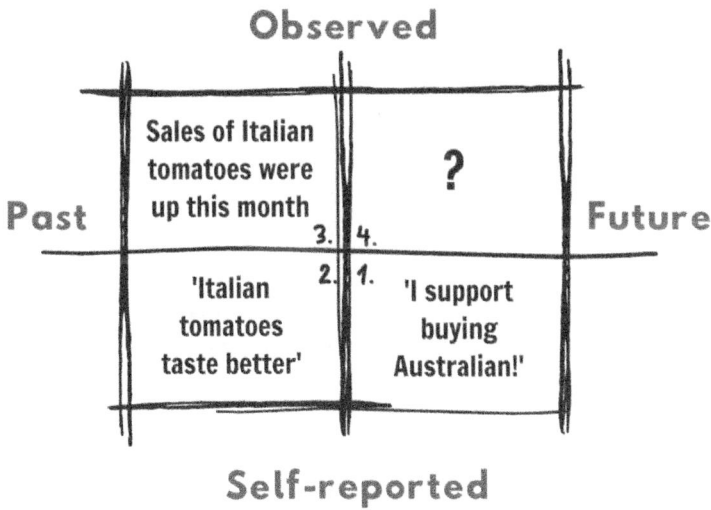

You are left with this question: how do you get people to buy Australian products even though there's a gap between what they say (1 and 2) and what they do (3)?

To address this (using future-oriented, observed behaviour (4)), you decide you will use the principle of social norms to counteract short-term bias (the immediate discount benefit). You build a campaign around why people who shop in this store buy tastier local produce, successfully counteracting the lure of cheap imports.

To map your own insights landscape see overleaf.

See also:

-> Trio of Truths About Your Customer, page 86
-> Two Speed Consumers, page 100

Mapping your insights landscape:

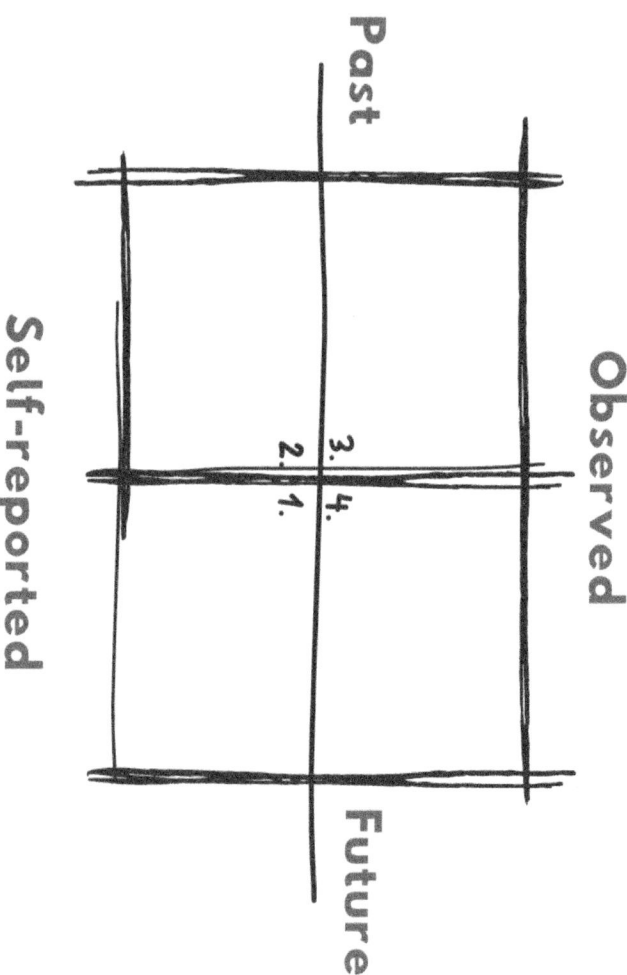

22. Trio of Truths About Your Customer

How your customers see themselves

This is about:

How your customer sees the world and their place in it.

Which is important because:

To influence action, you need to work with the story your customers tell themselves. If they can't integrate what you share with their pre-existing view, they will likely reject whatever you are suggesting.

It works like this:

Your customer is not a blank slate, waiting for you to share your wisdom. Instead:

1.   They write their own story about how the world works.
2.   They are the hero of that story.
3.   They run on batteries.

1. They write their story

Whatever you tell your customer will be slotted into their existing narrative about the world. It's as if they have scripted a TV series and you come along trying to insert a new storyline.

Known as the 'Narrative Fallacy', people tend to bind facts or events together even where no causal relationship exists. We like to join dots.

It means your customer will have a view of how the world works and will treat your perspective as something that either fits or does not. As a result, they are prone to:
• Seek information that confirms rather than disaffirms their view (i.e., Confirmation Bias), and
• Distort information that doesn't fit, in order to retain their sense of equilibrium (i.e., resolving cognitive dissonance).

To avoid rejection:
• **Understand their story**, listening for assumptions they make about their industry.
• Help them **uncover reasons** why the existing narrative is flawed

— this is grounds for you to provoke new thinking.

• Start **re-writing** the narrative, getting them to identify that the status quo is not perfect.

• Introduce a **new storyline** that they can easily integrate into their perspective.

For example:

Before I can get people to consider using behavioural economics, I must first get them to identify that there are flaws in how we currently think people behave. My training sessions deliberately start with a consideration of why we can't assume people are rational or rely on what people say they'll do. Only once they've acknowledged these problems exist can I introduce a new approach to resolve the challenge.

2. Your customer is the hero of their own story

Not only does your customer write the story, but they also make themselves the hero.

That means they will rationalise their beliefs and actions and be prone to:

• Act differently depending on whether they are anonymous or identifiable (i.e., Identity Bias).

• Excuse their poor behaviour if they are otherwise 'good' (i.e., Self-licensing).

• Internalise credit for their own success but blame the external situation for any missteps, whilst attributing reasons for the success and failure of others in the opposite direction (i.e., Fundamental Attribution Error).

To avoid hero issues:

- **Avoid diminishing or insulting** their sense of uniqueness (e.g., don't tell them 'Everybody is doing it, so you should too').
- Always approach the situation from a **'what's in it for them?'** perspective. Make them the hero.
- Presentations — proposals or seminars — will fail to engage if you talk about yourself too much at the start. Instead, lead with **insights about them** or their industry before introducing what you have to offer.
- Address them **by name** (e.g., 'Dear Sam' not 'Dear customer') and make sure you spell it correctly. While it sounds trivial, a misspelt name can greatly impair engagement.

For example:
- The first 75% of my proposals are all about the customer — their situation and how it can be resolved. I only include details about my credentials at the end, by which time they are curious.
- When asking your customer to do something (e.g., sign up to a newsletter), lead with the benefit to them (e.g., get 10% off) before what they have to do (e.g., provide their email).
- Your website needs to be about them, not you. Your history and philosophy makes you rather than them the hero, and should therefore be deprioritised. If your customer is truly interested, they'll explore your site to find it.

3. Your customer runs on batteries
Emotional and cognitive energy is limited, just like a battery. That means your customer will seek to conserve energy by following the path of least resistance wherever possible, and is prone to

making superficial expedient decisions (i.e., they are cognitively lazy). That means mostly good enough, 'satisficing' decisions rather than optimal, 'maximising' ones.

Being battery-powered means customers are likely to:
• Leave things as they are when they are fatigued.
• Rely more heavily on easy, quick, habitual thinking when they are tired and use deliberate, detail-oriented thinking only when they are well rested or when something is very important.
• Follow recommendations if they trust the person making them.

To work with your customer's battery, consider what state of energy you want them to be in?
• **High energy** can mean your customer will be open to considering what you are suggesting, but that can also invite more critical thinking.
• **Low energy** can mean a more passive audience, which can be good or bad depending on their mood. A passive, negatively disposed customer will not be bothered to contemplate change unless it is the easiest path to follow. A passive, positively inclined customer will tend to roll with your suggestions.

For example:
You schedule a meeting for an important decision first thing on a Monday morning. You schedule client coaching sessions on Fridays rather than Mondays because people are happier to talk about themselves (an easy topic) when their battery is depleted. You send an auto-renewal notice late on a Friday when people are more likely to let it roll over.

See also:

-> Zorro Technique, page 24
-> Conversational Cutlery, page 54
-> Fuzzy Future Self, page 96
-> Reactance Model, page 150

23. Hot-Cold Empathy Gap

How emotions govern decisions

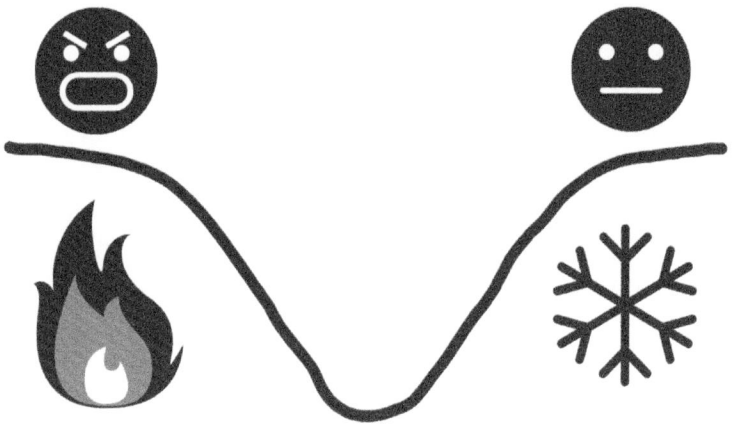

This is about:

The hot-cold empathy gap we have within ourselves.

Which is important because:

Our ability to forecast how we'll respond to something is impacted by the emotional state we are in at the time.

It works like this:

You have two settings, hot and cold.

• **Hot** state is when arousal is high. You're angry or agitated, hot and bothered.

• **Cold** state is when arousal is low. You are cool, calm and collected.

When you are in one state it is very difficult to imagine the other, so you over or underestimate how you'll behave. In a cold state, you forget how pressure changes things. In a hot state, you forget about the promises you made to act in a particular way.

All is not lost though, because by anticipating the hot-cold empathy gap you can engineer ways of behaving in a way you want to when the moment arises.

For example:

It's the start of a new year and you decide (in a cold state) to overhaul your diet, promising you won't eat junk food anymore. A few weeks later you are feeling overworked, hormonal and tired (hot state) so you reach for pizza and beer. The better approach when you are in a cold state, is to anticipate you will feel run down at times and have healthier options on hand.

You are busy at work and under significant pressure (hot state). To keep a project moving you take some short cuts, thinking you'll get the proper sign-offs later. Six months down the track, your boss pulls you aside and asks you to explain why you breached procurement guidelines. As much as you try to describe the pressure you were under at the time, the rationalisations you make in your current cold state seem flimsy.

The better approach, when finding yourself in an overwhelmed hot state, is to imagine yourself explaining this decision in a few months' time, or from the witness box. This will pour cold water over your hot state and help you make better decisions in the moment.

See also:

-> Partitioning Principle, page 66
-> Trio of Truths About Your Customer, page 86
-> Fuzzy Future Self, page 96

24. Fuzzy Future Self

Why now trumps later

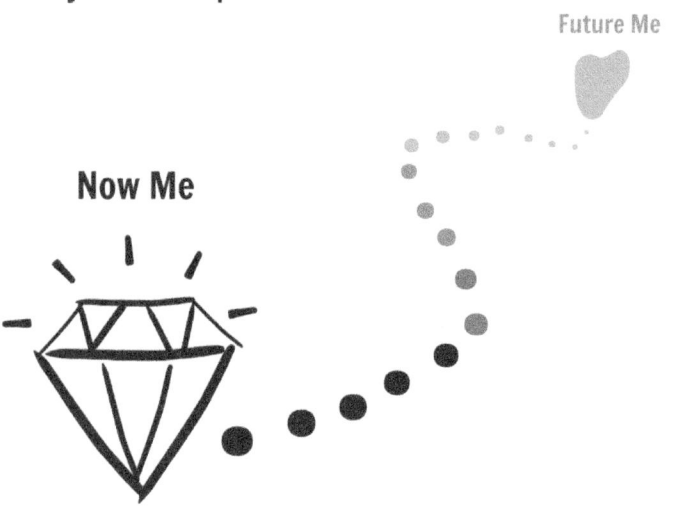

Future Me

Now Me

This is about:

Convincing customers to act now for something that won't benefit them until later on.

Which is important because:

We often use future benefits to convince people to do something now and wonder why we don't succeed. It's because we've failed to cut through a bias humans have for the present. What matters now, matters most.

We see this with macro issues, like climate change, and micro issues, like buying expensive shoes rather than saving for retirement.

The challenge in business is trying to get people to engage with our products, services or ideas, when many have an immediate cost (money, time, effort), but no immediate payoff.

It works like this:

We have two versions of ourselves — Now Me and Future Me. The needs and desires of Now Me are as clear cut as a 6-carat diamond. Your Now Me wants to enjoy pleasure and avoid pain, so anything uncomfortable or undesirable is kicked down the road where Future Me will have to deal with it. If there's no immediate benefit, Now Me is not interested.

You are able to load Future Me up with all this unpleasantness because, for all intents and purposes, Future Me is a stranger — a fuzzy, distant, unfamiliar blob for whom you have little interest or empathy.

You also imbue your Future Me with all sorts of virtue that your Now Me just doesn't possess. Of course, you promise yourself, Future Me will definitely eat better, exercise more and read the complete works of Virginia Woolf. Now Me, however, has had a hard day and deserves to sit on the couch and eat ice cream.

Your task — in business and in life — is to bridge the temporal divide and get Now Me to act for Future Me's benefit.

For example:

When enticing people to sign-up to your newsletter so they can learn something (future benefit), give them an immediate reward for bothering (like a discount or instant gift).

When asking stakeholders to prioritise investment in your project, (which won't generate financial returns for many years), look for an immediate benefit for them. Perhaps they'll be relieved to have the project locked in at current prices, or checked off their to-do list? Will this give them access to the latest technology or something they can brag about to peers? Is it something they'll appreciate including on their resume?

See also:

-> Williams Behaviour Change Model, page 8

-> Timing Rewards, page 34

-> Decision-Action Conversion, page 68

-> Trio of Truths About Your Customer, page 86

-> Hot-Cold Empathy Gap, page 92

-> Momentum Model, page 158

25. Two Speed Consumers

Slowing the speed of change

This is about:

The illusion that customer needs are always changing.

Which is important because:

A lot of businesses assume people operate at only one speed — fast. That customers are always chasing the new thing, the shiniest object and the latest trend.

This is 'shiny toy' syndrome means you end up in a cycle of trying to divine what's next. What's the next social media craze, yo-yo/ fidget spinner/fidget popper or crypto currency? Should you shift marketing activities from Instagram to TikTok? Is it worth building product for that new platform or will it fade out quickly like

Clubhouse or Twitter Spaces?

Your days feel like a game of 'whack-a-mole'. Just when you think you have things sorted, something new pops up.

The way to get ahead of the curve and slow things down — without actually slowing them down — is to dispel the illusion.

Because while there is an incessant thirst for the new, that's only part of the story. People don't operate at one speed; they operate at two.

It's not only about what changes, it's also about what *doesn't*. Human wiring. People 10 years ago, 20 years ago or 100 years ago made decisions in largely the same way as we do today.

It works like this:

Focus less on what does change, and more on what does not. Humans are wired to be lazy (we like to conserve mental energy), scared (we like to avoid risk) and confused (we can get easily overwhelmed). Just knowing this will help you feel like the world has slowed down. You'll have more space and clarity to make decisions. You'll design better solutions. You'll stop jumping at shadows.

For example:

We think of Instagram as a relatively new thing, but seeking social approval certainly isn't. In 1862, for example, John Solomon commissioned oil paintings of himself and his wife in order to change perceptions of his family. As the son of notorious thief Ikey Solomon, John wanted to stave off reputational damage and reset the family narrative. While pixels have replaced paint in the modern age, the hard-wired motivations are the same.

See also:

-> Williams Behaviour Change Model, page 8
-> Trio of Truths About Your Customer, page 86
-> BE-gmentation, page 118
-> Designing Mindset, page 138

26. Me-TT Model

How context shapes behaviour

Me   **Them**   **There**

This is about:

Optimising the three contexts that shape behaviour: Me (personal), Them (social) and There (environmental).

Which is important because:

Aside from inherent traits, people's decisions are influenced by context — who is around them and where they are.

It works like this:

When assessing how best to influence behaviour, do a quick audit of the three contexts that shape decisions so you optimise each. This is the Me-TT Model.

1. Me — 'Me' Context: How your customer is naturally geared

These are the core behavioural tendencies that would govern decision making even when alone on a desert island. Your customer will have these tendencies without seeing your marketing or visiting your shop, and even before they know how other people feel about you.

Me context wiring means your customers are impacted by things such as:
• Status Quo Bias – leaving things as they are rather than changing.
• Loss Aversion – avoiding loss rather than seeking gain.
• Short-term Bias – wanting instant gratification.
• Mood Heuristic – their feelings impact their decisions.

To shape the Me context, **ask yourself**: What's their current situation? What do they have to give up to incorporate what you are suggesting? Is it immediately gratifying? How can you make them feel good about this decision?

For example:

You are a salesperson in an electronics store. Realising your customers are prone to immediate gratification, you mention how you can arrange delivery of their new TV that very afternoon.

2. T — 'Them' context: How your customer is impacted by others

Instead of being alone on a desert island, thankfully we are usually surrounded by people. The Them context is about how your customer's behaviour is impacted by others.

Them behavioural tendencies include:

• Social proof – seeking evidence of what others have done or approve of.

• Herding – when in doubt following what others have done.

• Authority – being persuaded by those in authority.

• Uniqueness – seeking to maintain individuality.

To shape the Them context, **ask yourself**: What do your customers see others doing? How will doing business with you affect their status? Whose authority will be persuasive? How can you ensure they feel unique rather than just another number?

For example:

When talking your customer through which TV to buy, you use your authority as an expert to recommend the one you believe best meets their needs. You also mention it has been one of the most popular sellers.

3. T — 'There' context: How your customer is impacted by their environment

Of the three domains, the 'There' context is the one over which you have most control. You can design your digital or physical environment to shape your customer's decision — e.g., using lighting, sounds, packaging materials, shelving, and price ticketing to optimise your chance of influencing action.

There context behavioural tendencies include:

• Priming – contextual cues that influence people to act in a certain way without being consciously aware of them (e.g., background traffic noise prompting people to buy car insurance).

• Framing – customers are persuaded by how information is presented (e.g., 2% fat vs 98% fat free).

• Choice overload – customers love the freedom to choose but can get overwhelmed by it.

• Relativity – value is relative not absolute, so $10 for a glass of wine at a restaurant is different to $10 for a bottle at the liquor shop because the context is different.

• Anchoring – customers are persuaded by values that may not even relate to what they are looking to buy (e.g., a $500,000 Rolls-Royce seems inexpensive when it is sold amongst multi-million-dollar cruisers at a boat show).

To shape the There context, **ask yourself**: How is your customer impacted by the environment in which they are deciding and consuming your product? E.g., lighting, smells, noise, temperature, packaging, whether alternatives are available, your branding, your choice of typeface? Is there a different way you can describe your offer to frame it to advantage? What cues are you providing about whether you are a price sensitive shop (e.g., Electronics retailer JB Hi-Fi, which deliberately makes everything look like it's on sale) or high end (e.g., Apple, which is rarely on sale).

For example:
When talking with your customer about price, you mention that the particular TV they are looking at was $800 and now is only $650, anchoring their perception of value.

See also:
-> Williams Behaviour Change Model, page 8
-> Behavioural Models Overview, page 16
-> Trio of Truths About Your Customer, page 86

27. Empathy Map

How to shift into your customer's perspective

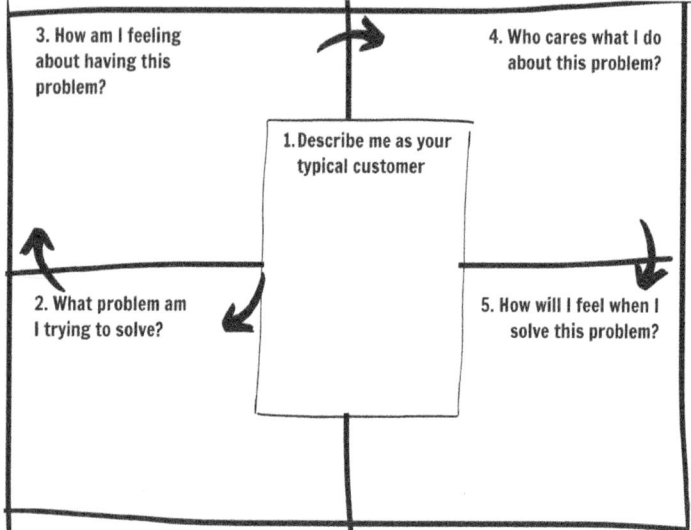

3. How am I feeling about having this problem?

4. Who cares what I do about this problem?

1. Describe me as your typical customer

2. What problem am I trying to solve?

5. How will I feel when I solve this problem?

This is about:

Getting into your customer's headspace.

Which is important because:

Seeing a situation from your customer's point of view will help you influence more effectively because you'll be more likely to focus on their needs, not yours. Your empathy will come through in how and what you communicate.

It works like this:

Complete the Empathy Map with what you (think you) know about your customer. You will have to make assumptions, and that's okay. The answers don't have to be right, necessarily. Going through the exercise will be enough to reveal new insights about your customers and what you offer them.

1.   Describe me as your typical customer

Here you can add any defining characteristics or demographics about your customer. Who are they (likely to be)? Is it an individual or a group?

2.   What problem am I trying to solve?

Describe what they are grappling with. What answers are they searching for? What are they Googling? What's on their mind?

3.   How am I feeling about having this problem?

This will help you get into their emotional state. Are they energised? Stressed? Overawed? Frustrated? Are they waking up at night in terror or daydreaming about the possibilities?

4.   Who cares what I do about this problem?

People are influenced by others, directly or indirectly. They are likely to need to explain or share their decision with their boss, their bank manager, or their loved ones, so it helps if you build a story to convince these stakeholders, as well.

5.   How will I feel when I solve this problem?

Again, this will help you get into their emotional state once the problem has been resolved. Will they be relieved? Happy? Relaxed? Clever? This is the true payoff for proceeding with what you are suggesting.

For example:

Imagine you are a superannuation provider who wants to get younger professionals to contribute additional funds to their retirement savings.

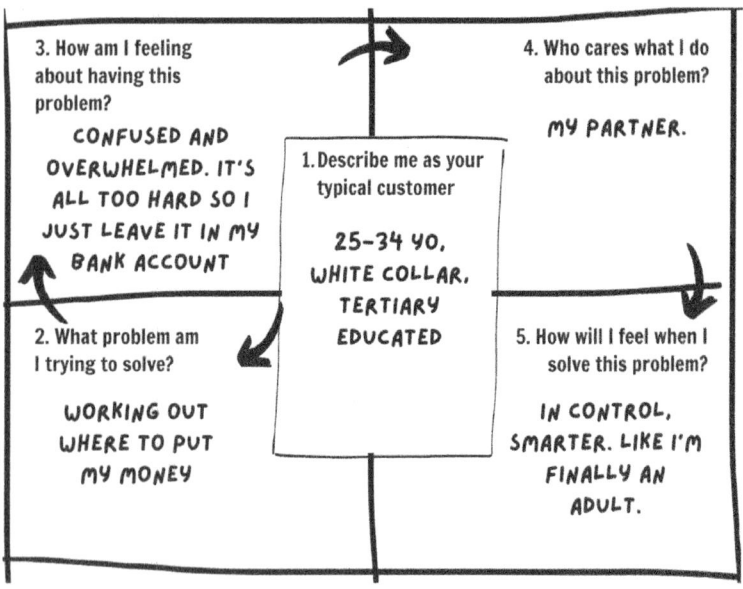

PART 3.

MODELS FOR TARGETING BY TYPE

How to match your approach to your audience

28. Personality Profiling Tools

How to work out which profiling tool is right for you

Reliability

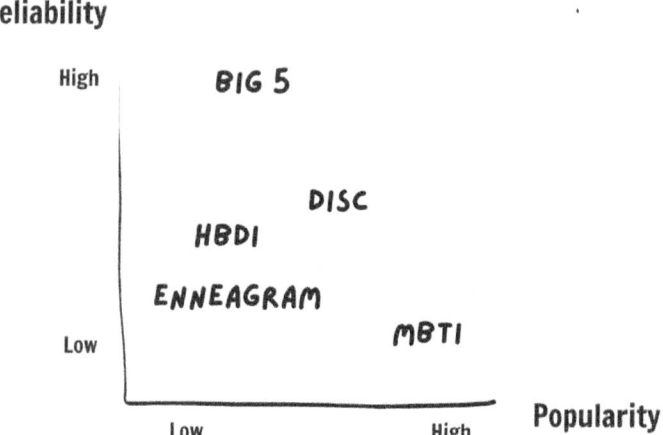

This is about:

Identifying which personality profiling tool might be best.

Which is important because:

Personality profiling tools don't come cheap. There are many different tools and it can be difficult to know which to use. Each tool has pros and cons, advocates and detractors.

Personality profiling tools are typically survey-based questionnaires that seek to identify an individual's inherent traits.

By revealing your thinking or communication preferences, for example, the theory is you can work on your strengths and weaknesses or relate better with others.

Some of the tools most commonly used include:
- The **Big 5** personality traits (Openness, Conscientiousness, Extraversion, Agreeableness, Neuroticism, also known as OCEAN and the Five Factor Model)
- **DISC** profile (Dominance, Influence, Steadiness and Conscientiousness)
- **HBDI** (Herrmann-Brain Dominance Instrument)
- The **Enneagram**
- **MBTI** (Myers-Briggs Type Indicator)

It works like this:

We can plot the various personality profiling tools according to two factors: popularity and reliability. I've done this according to my own understanding of the tools, but you may decide to create your own version using these or other criteria. Be guided by what you want the tool to do for you.

Popularity means how mainstream and widely adopted they are, and **reliability**, how likely you are to get the same result when you retake the test.

Ideally, you'd want a tool that rates highly on both because that means it gives you accurate results and is commonly referenced across different businesses. Unfortunately, no one tool seems to meet this ideal.

example:

The Myers-Briggs Type Indicator (MBTI) is hugely popular but has questionable reliability. That means your classification might change when you retake the assessment. The Big 5 is less popular but highly regarded for its reliability.

See also:

-> Customer Insights Landscape, page 80
-> Trio of Truths About Your Customer, page 86

29. BE-gmentation

Why similarities should come before differences

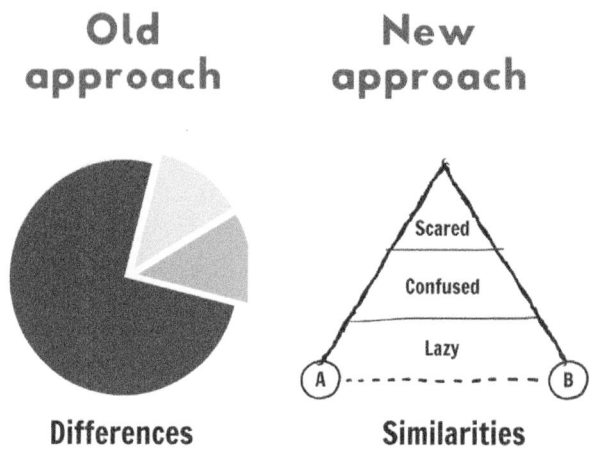

Old approach	New approach
Differences	Similarities

This is about:

When and how to segment your market to get your product or marketing to best engage your customers.

Which is important because:

You might be slicing and dicing your market too soon, missing out on economies of scale. By starting with the universals — what applies to all of your audience, you can get the biggest bang for buck.

It works like this:

The old way of doing things was to dive into differences between groups based on things like age, income or life stage. 'Customer personas' (avatars) would often result.

The problem with segmenting too soon is you have to take each segment profile in turn and run them through the universal behaviours. Not only is this repetitious, but it also means that you lose the 'low hanging fruit' common across all segments.

The better approach is to start with similarities, not differences. Rather than asking 'what makes customers different from one another?', ask 'what makes them the same?'

I call this behavioural economics segmentation, or 'BE-gmentation'.

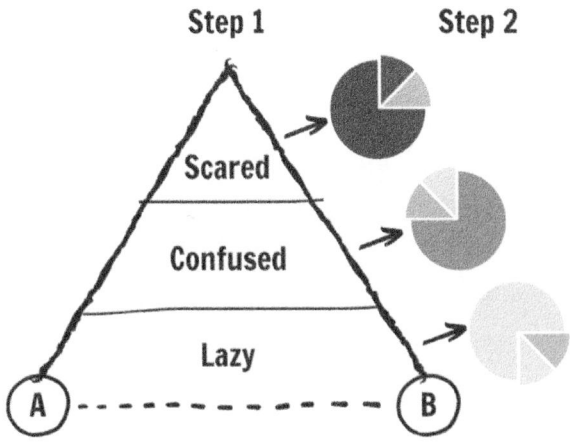

Step 1. Similarities

Start with the foundations of human behaviour — that people are lazy, scared and confused (page 8). This ensures you are covering the three core reasons people won't engage with or act on your message or initiative.

Step 2. Differences

Once you've explored the universals you can move to the nuance — what distinguishes people (or groups) from one another. This will help you craft a message or initiative to resonate best with a particular group within your market.

For example:

Let's say you are devising an initiative to get college students to eat less pizza (i.e., addressing the laziness barrier to behaviour). You decide to use 'social norms' because most people, regardless of life stage, are prone to being influenced by others.

Your question then becomes, which others are these students most influenced by?

That's where segmentation will help because people are more likely to be influenced by people like them — their 'in-group'.

Students of 'blue' university will respond better if the message comes from fellow blue-tonians for example, rather than representatives of 'red' university, even though the campaign structure and core message can be the same across both populations.

See also:

-> Williams Behaviour Change Model, page 8
-> Customer Insights Landscape, page 80
-> Influencing Individuals Vs. Groups, page 122

30. Influencing Individuals Vs. Groups

How familiarity and group size affects influence

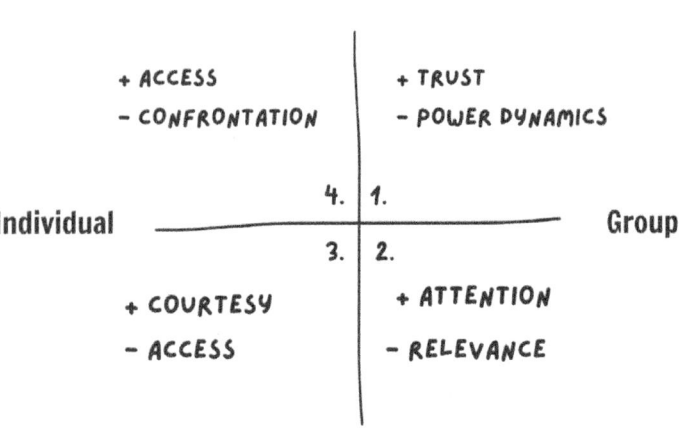

Familiar

+ ACCESS
- CONFRONTATION

+ TRUST
- POWER DYNAMICS

4. | 1.

Individual   Group

3. | 2.

+ COURTESY
- ACCESS

+ ATTENTION
- RELEVANCE

Unfamiliar

This is about:

The number of people you are influencing (one Vs. many), and how familiar they are.

Which is important because:

Your approach may need to change depending on how many people you are trying to influence and the expectations the relationship comes with.

When it comes to influencing **groups**, the biggest upside is scale — the sheer weight of numbers. However, you will have to manage dynamics within the group and the tendency for freeloading, which is when people feel they can hide behind the efforts of others.

Individuals have the advantage of heightened engagement — it's harder for them to hide. However, it can feel more confronting, for both you and them.

Familiarity is both a blessing and curse. The upside is you gain access, the downside is the relationship comes with baggage.

It works like this:

1.   Familiar + group

If a group is **familiar** with you (and you with them), they are more likely to trust you. You are part of the 'in-group' so they will be less likely to have their guard up. You can get to the point quicker.

However, with familiarity comes existing power dynamics, and these can work against your ability to influence. You will be pegged to some form of hierarchy, where some will think you are subordinate, while others defer to your positional power.

To influence them, use the credibility you already have with the group and your insights into the prevailing dynamics and issues. Focus your efforts on getting those who other people follow onside first.

For example:

You are a team leader trying to get staff to adhere to a new policy. You call people together and run them through an exercise (such as the Zorro technique, page 24) where you first build an appetite for changing things (e.g., we seem to agree that doing it the old way has more problems than we realised!) before talking through what the new policy is.

2.   Unfamiliar + group

When a group is **unfamiliar** with you (and you with them), they are likely to be a little wary because you haven't yet built trust. First impressions are important because they will judge you in those initial moments.

To influence the group, use your outsider status and 'fresh pair of eyes' to establish authority. They will respond better if you work 'with' them rather than have something done 'to' them, so make sure you emphasise why what you are talking about is relevant to them.

For example:

You're a consultant kicking off a project and your aim is to gain buy-in and trust. You start the engagement by contextualising your involvement (e.g., industry changes, the pressures they're under) before briefly credentialing yourself (e.g., area of expertise and track record) and, most importantly, working with them to identify why this project is relevant to them. This is about gaining their buy-in.

3.   Unfamiliar + individual

When it comes to **individuals**, if they are not familiar with you the challenge will be gaining access in the first place. It's easy to fob off a stranger who cold calls, for example.

Once you do gain access, you will probably both be on your best behaviour, treading carefully. Don't mistake their politeness for agreement, though. They may simply not want to be rude in refusing you.

Your aim in this situation is to gain their interest and establish your credibility. That means doing what you say you'll do and not pushing too hard. Give without expecting to get anything in return. This helps you build goodwill which they may eventually reciprocate.

For example:

Sending a LinkedIn request: 'Hi <name>, I've been following your work for a while now and have been impressed by x. I'm hoping we can connect?' or 'Hi <name>, I see you are in the x industry like I am. In case it's of interest, I've included a link to an article in (publication) I found really interesting. I hope you do too, and that you'd be happy to connect with me?'

4.   Familiar + individual

Trying to influence someone who is familiar to and with you is its own challenge. Yes, you can probably gain access to them but there is more at stake. There is nowhere to hide, so it can feel confrontational, particularly if you are asking them to change their way of doing things.

Your aim is to get them to think what you are proposing is their idea. Bring to mind things they themselves have said about the issue so they feel heard and that what you are suggesting is consistent with their perspective.

For example:

Trying to table a new initiative with a stakeholder: 'I've been reflecting on what you said about x the other day and was hoping we could talk about it a bit further?', or 'Your perspective on x really resonated with me. What were your thoughts if we started to consider y?'

See also:

-> Zorro Technique, page 24
-> The Porter Principle, page 32
-> Conversational Cutlery, page 54
-> Empathy Map, page 108

Mapping your audience:

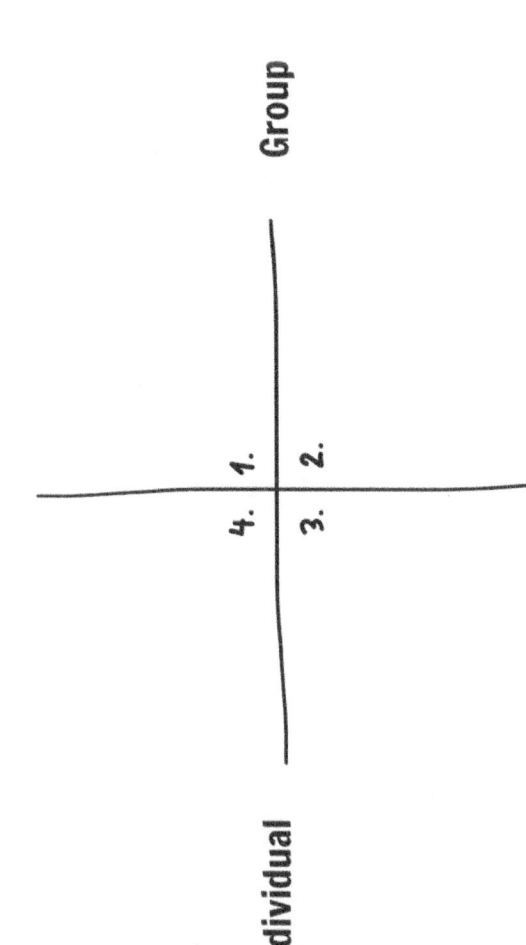

31. 360 Degree BE

Where to use behavioural influence

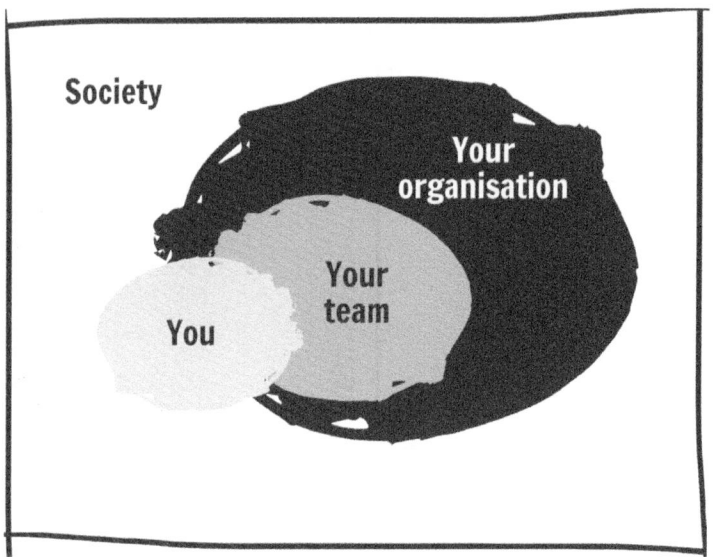

This is about:

Using your knowledge of behavioural economics (BE) to influence people across multiple domains.

Which is important because:

We tend to think influencing skills are only relevant for customer or staff interactions when they can apply in all facets of life.

It works like this:

There are at least four contexts in which you can apply behavioural influencing techniques:

• **You** – influencing yourself to behave in a different way, like eating more healthily or exercising more regularly.

• **Your team** – influencing members of your team to work differently.

• **Your organisation** – influencing stakeholders, colleagues, suppliers and customers to do what you'd like them to do.

• **Society** – influencing family and friends and people in your community.

For example:

You learn that we are 'lazy, scared and confused' and start to use the Williams Behaviour Change Model (page 8) to address behaviours in your life.

• **You** – You identify 'laziness' is getting in the way of you cooking healthy meals when you finish work, so start leaving the chopping board on the benchtop. Having it there makes you more inclined to chop vegetables and once you've done that, it's easy to throw a stir fry together most nights.

• **Your team** – You realise that the reason your team are not following directions is you haven't been clear on what you need them to do (they are 'confused'). You now start emails and meetings by making sure your objective is clear.

• **Your organisation** – You work out that the stakeholder who is dodging your calls is worried (i.e., 'scared') about agreeing to your project in case it goes wrong. You reassure them they will not be held responsible for the outcome and are able to gain their support.

· **Society** – Property developers are threatening to knock down a building with cultural significance, so you set about galvanising the local community by outlining what they stand to lose if the developers proceed (i.e., using 'scared' to overcome 'lazy').

See also:

-> Williams Behaviour Change Model, page 8
-> Williams Behaviour Change Venn, page 20
-> Me-TT Model, page 104
-> Influencing Individuals Vs. Groups, page 122

32. Arming Your Advocate

Helping customers convince others

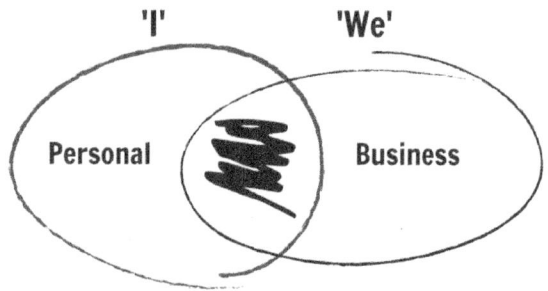

This is about:

Helping your customer convince other people, like their boss, team or a family member, that they should proceed. I call this 'arming your advocate'.

Which is important because:

Sometimes a customer you think is keen goes cold once they have to justify the decision to someone else.

It works like this:

A customer who needs to convince others will have both 'I' concerns and 'we' concerns.

· 'I' concerns are about what they want out of this transaction.

· **'We'** concerns are business (or family) considerations.

When making 'I' decisions, people most commonly use their feelings. How do they feel about you? About this? Will it make them look good? Feel good?

When convincing others in a 'we' decision, they tend to use facts because they expect greater scrutiny of their recommendation.

That means you need to help them strike a balance between a personal and business rationale, arming them with what they need to explain the decision to their stakeholders. What can they use to substantiate their choice and avoid any sense they're doing this just because it 'feels' right?

For example:

You are selling software to a new business client. In your initial conversations, take an interest in them, their role and their insights into their organisation. This will establish rapport and mean they are more likely to like you and feel good about your proposal. You can talk about how implementing the new software will help their personal priorities and professional development (e.g., ticking a task off their to-do list, status from bringing new technology in and 'shaking things up', looking for new approaches across industry).

Once you get the sense that they are on board, your attention can turn to who else will be involved in the decision and what they'll need to be convinced. The emphasis with 'we' decisions is aligning the proposal with the business' strategic priorities. Seed soundbites your customer can use when discussing the proposal with their colleagues (e.g., it saved XYZ company the equivalent of 2 weeks of work in the first quarter), and make sure they have answers for any possible objections. Provide collateral that covers relevant facts, figures and credentials too, so you look credible.

See also:

-> Trio of Truths About Your Customer, page 86
-> Empathy Map, page 108
-> Influencing Individuals Vs. Groups, page 122

PART 4.

MODELS FOR IMPROVING COMMUNICATIONS

How to craft effective messages

33. Designing Mindset

How to design for your customer

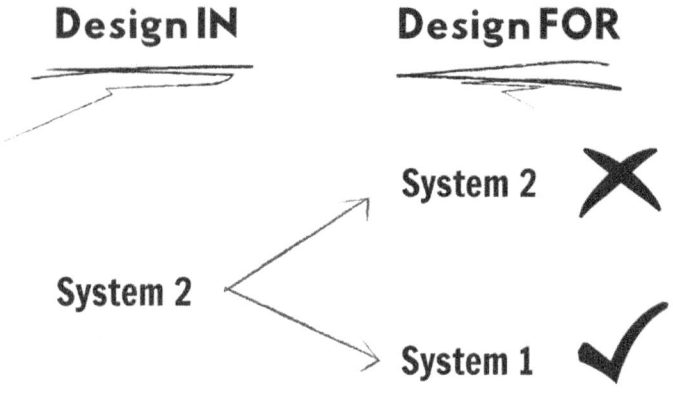

This is about:

Designing product or marketing for how your customer will likely receive it.

Which is important because:

Our influencing efforts fail when we design for idealised rather than real behaviour. The mindset we design IN is different to the mindset we need to design FOR.

It works like this:

When you design something, like a new product or piece of communications, you are using 'System 2', slow thinking. System 2 is the metaphor used by psychologist and Nobel Laureate, Daniel Kahneman to describe the cognitive processes we use when focusing on details and logic.

The trap is you can get so close to what you are creating that you lose sight of how a customer is likely to view it. You assume they'll see what you see, and value the features you value. In essence, you assume they'll care about it as much as you do, using their System 2 slow, rational processing to consider what you're suggesting.

Instead, they'll likely be using 'System 1', lazy processing. They'll judge it on how they feel, how much effort is involved and whether it looks like a good deal.

While you can't stop yourself from designing in a System 2 way, you need to create for your customer's System 1*.

---

*There are occasions when you may want to design for System 2 processing. For example, drivers are becoming increasingly passive and tuning out of the task of driving (relying on System 1) because vehicles automate so much. After a while, we don't hear all the beeps and alarms.

For example:

When you design *for* System 2, your work will tend to assume the customer will read a text in full rather than skipping over sentences and that they'll be deeply interested in you. Communications tend to be text heavy and poorly formatted, products rely on instruction manuals to function, interfaces are clunky, and workplace policies expect people will remember detailed work instructions. In a nutshell, designing for System 2 overestimates how much people will bother thinking about something.

E.g., most Terms and Conditions policies.

When you design *for* System 1, instructions can be understood at a glance, products are easy to unbox and start using, communications draw attention to the most important information or action, and new behaviours feel familiar because they're built on existing ones. In short, you design for lazy thinking.

E.g., Apple iPhone, Amazon 1-click

See also:

-> Williams Behaviour Change Model, page 8
-> Williams Behaviour Change Venn, page 20
-> Trio of Truths About Your Customer, page 86
-> Effective Emails, page 146

141

...ails Get Ignored

Why staff ignore your emails

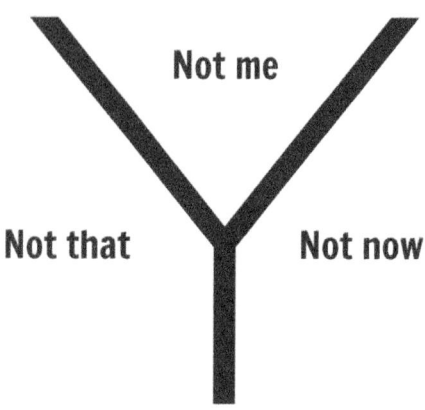

This is about:

A communications paradox in business where staff complain that their bosses never tell them anything, while bosses believe that staff are being bombarded with information.

Which is important because:

We spend a disproportionate amount of time writing and receiving emails. Clearly it is a waste of everyone's valuable time if important messages are ignored.

It works like this:

The reality, when staff tell you that they're not feeling informed by your communications, is that it is usually a problem of perception.

You may be 'informing' them, but they don't perceive it that way. A bit like Teflon, the message doesn't stick. They ignore you because we have a relevance problem, and that's a result of three communications mistakes:

Not me

When your message doesn't spell out why it's relevant to that person. It may be relevant, but it doesn't come across that way.

Not now

Messages that are about the past or too far into the future are less likely to feel relevant, and less likely to be remembered. I care less if it's not about now.

Not that

Perhaps most irritating of all, a message that should be relevant but isn't helpful at all. In fact, it may create more confusion and uncertainty than it seeks to address.

For example:

To address these three issues, you need to get into the headspace of the intended recipient and write from their point of view.

- **Why?** What's the behavioural objective? What's the behaviour we want to see? Do we want them to do something as a result, or do nothing?
- **Who?** Who is this for? Is it 'do something' for some people but 'do nothing' for others? Remember, we want to avoid a 'Not Me' reaction.
- **How?** How is it best communicated? This includes the channel, tone and who it comes from (the messenger).
- **When?** When will it land best with the audience you are trying to influence? Time of day? Time of week? Time of year? This is about avoiding a 'Not Now' response.
- **What?** What's the substance of your message? How will you pull it together to make sure it is relevant, engaging, and meaningful? This is to avoid 'Not that'.

See also:

-> Trio of Truths About Your Customer, page 86
-> Fuzzy Future Self, page 96
-> Empathy Map, page 108
-> Effective Emails, page 146

‌‍ɛrfective Emails

How to write emails that work

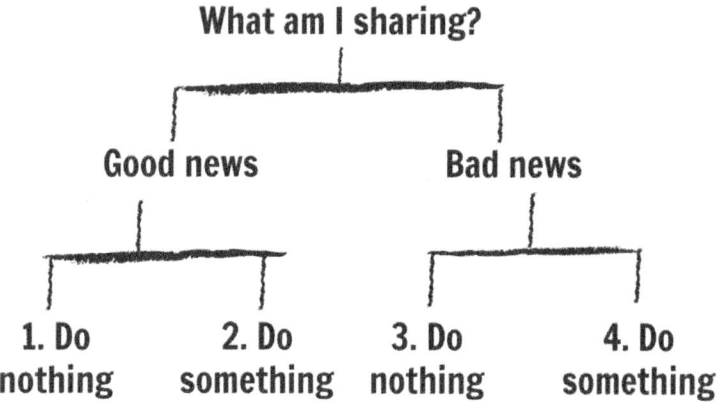

What am I sharing?

Good news — Bad news

1. Do nothing | 2. Do something | 3. Do nothing | 4. Do something

This is about:

Writing emails that get the response you want.

Which is important because:

We waste time writing emails that get ignored, or worse, provoke a negative reaction.

It works like this:

First ask, is the news you are sharing with your customer good news or bad news for them?

If it is good news, the tone can be upbeat and positive. If it is bad news, you'll need to tread more carefully.

Then ask, what do you want them to do as a result of reading your email? Do you want them to do something (action required) or do nothing (no action required)?

If you don't need (or want) them to do anything, tell them that so they feel reassured. This closes the communication loop so they are not left wondering what to do next.

If you want them to do something, the 'why' of doing so must be clear along with the 'how' to do it.

For example:

1.   Good news, Do Nothing

You're holding their price at last year's levels rather than increasing it. Build goodwill by telling them why you've decided to do this (e.g., we've decided to absorb…), and reassure them their service will remain unchanged.

2.   Good news, Do something

You're giving them access to a bonus product but they'll need to click the button to claim it. Frame it as a customer benefit so they understand why they are receiving this benefit (e.g., to thank you, to celebrate…) and make the call-to-action (CTA) as simple as possible to use. Let them know why they won't want to miss out on this special offer.

3.   Bad news, Do nothing

You're increasing their price and will amend the amount billed automatically. Start by briefly contextualising the reason for the price adjustment before assuring them you'll take care of the change — there is nothing they need to do. While your objective is to minimise the chances of a negative reaction and customer complaints, you should provide an avenue for them to contact you if they need to.

4.   Bad news, Do something

You're discontinuing the product they are using and need them to switch to an alternative. Explain the reason for the change before moving to what they need to do. Ideally you would provide a recommendation (e.g., based on x we suggest y) and explain what happens if they don't take action (i.e. if we don't hear from you, we'll move you across to z).

See also:

-> Effort Vs. Reward Equation, page 28
-> Customer Retention Strategies, page 62
-> Empathy Map, page 108
-> Y Emails Get Ignored, page 142
-> Reactance Model, page 150
-> Rage-O-Meter, page 164

36. Reactance Model

How to avoid your influencing efforts backfiring

Reactance   Compliance

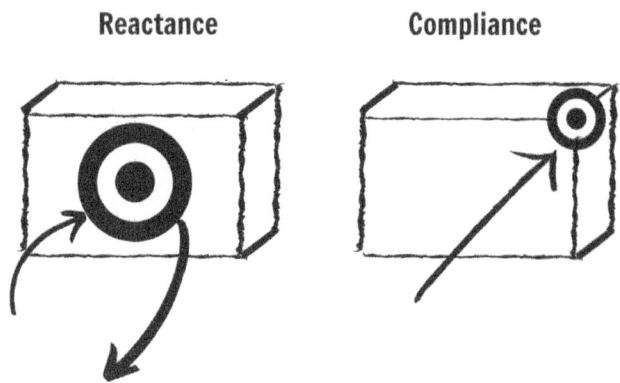

This is about:

Telling a customer they should do something, and them doing the opposite instead.

Which is important because:

No one wins when a customer refuses to do or accept something that would benefit them. You miss out and they do too.

It works like this:

When people feel their decision-making freedom or personal autonomy is threatened, they try to reassert themselves by moving in the opposite direction. This is known as 'reactance'.

Think of carving a block of stone. If you hit the stone straight on, your chisel will react by bouncing off.

You may inadvertently trigger reactance by:
· Telling them what they should do
· Watching them as they shop
· Sending unsolicited, highly personalised emails (i.e., it feels creepy because you know too much about them)
· Sending generic, non-personalised emails (i.e., you should know more about them and they feel they are being treated as a number)
· Introducing pop-up online ads that interfere with their intended task; and
· Making unsolicited product recommendations while they shop online (i.e., you don't know what I want!).

To avoid reactance, we instead need to chip away at the corners of our block of stone.. Position what you are asking from their point of view and give them a sense of control over the decision. And, if you are like me, you'll want to point out how much you have in common because similarity has been found to reduce reactance, too. (See what I did there?)

For example:

When making a recommendation, couch it as follows: 'It's your decision of course, but what I've found with other clients in a similar position is...', 'Totally up to you, but if it were me I would...', or 'Feel free to say no, but I was thinking...'

See also:

-> Trio of Truths About Your Customer, page 86
-> Empathy Map, page 108
-> Designing Mindset, page 138
-> Zero-Sum is Dumb, page 162

37. Frame the Gain Vs. Loss is Boss

When to go negative

Gain

'RETAIN MORE CUSTOMERS...'	'GAIN MORE CUSTOMERS...'
'EARN HIGHER INTEREST...'	'GET A 10% DISCOUNT...'

Existing — 4. | 1. — New

3. | 2.

| 'AVOID LOSING CUSTOMERS' | 'DON'T MISS OUT ON NEW CUSTOMERS' |
| 'STOP WASTING MONEY ON FEES...' | 'DON'T BE LEFT BEHIND...' |

Loss

This is about:

Eliciting the desired response from your customer by using positive and negative framing in the right way.

Which is important because:

Gains and losses do not have the same emotional resonance. Gains are often seen as 'nice to haves', whereas losses are 'must avoids'.

It works like this:

First consider whether the gain or loss frame will be more influential. The technical term is a 'promotion' Vs. 'prevention' focus, where **promotion** emphasises the upside (the gain, benefit, win), and **prevention**, the downside (the loss, risk, disadvantage).

'You can save' uses promotion framing, whereas 'avoid wasting' uses prevention.

In your desire to be positive, you might default to promotion (gain) focus, but this doesn't mean it's the most effective approach.

Alongside the gain/loss framing, consider whether the situation relates to a new or existing circumstance.

When it relates to an **existing** circumstance, like if they have an incumbent supplier or use the type of product you sell, you can use 'sunk cost' to create tension. In other words, they may not be getting the most from the investment their business has already made.

If it is **new** to them, you can instead emphasise what they are missing out by not having it (prevention focus, e.g., 'don't be left behind') or what they stand to gain (promotion focus, e.g., 'save time', 'save money').

For example:

For a new client who doesn't yet use products like yours, you decide to use promotion framing in one campaign: 'Get the edge on your competitors', and prevention framing in another: 'Avoid losing market share'.

For a client who uses your competitor's product, you create tension with prevention framing ('A lot of people in your industry are struggling with outdated technology') before talking about the gains they can enjoy ('We can save you time and money').

	Existing Have already made an investment of time, money or resources	**New** Haven't yet invested in this area, untapped opportunity
Promotion Gain, grow, win, save	• 'Save time/money on your xyz technology'	• 'Gain market share' • 'Save time by…'
Prevention Avoid losing/wasting/missing out on	• 'Is your x working as hard as it should for you?' • 'Stop wasting time'	• 'Don't get left behind' • 'Mistakes to avoid when looking to…"'

See also:

-> PES-imistic Paradigm, page 38
-> Effective Emails page 146
-> Zero-Sum is Dumb, page 162

38. Momentum Model

Finishing on a high

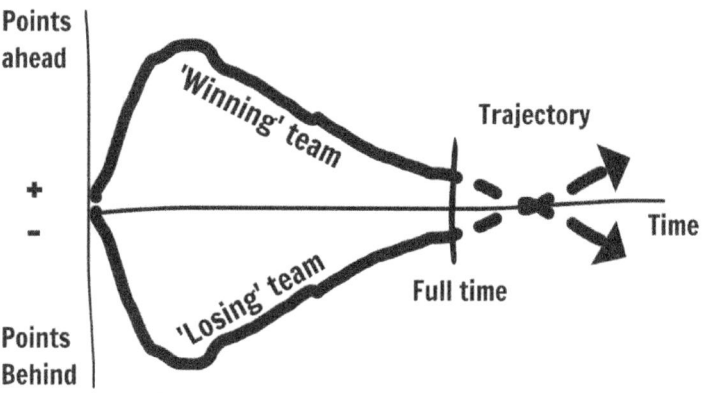

This is about:

Results being about *when*, not just *what*.

Which is important because:

A financial year that starts well but ends with a whimper can make it seem like things are going badly, whereas results that build momentum and end on a high can make things seem great.

It works like this:

A funny thing happens in the wash-up of a sporting contest. A team that dominates early, has their lead narrowed throughout the match, and clings on to win is often seen as having 'lost'. Their victory is described in negative terms like 'just managed to hang on', 'squandered their lead' or 'fell away'.

A team that comes from behind to almost snatch victory, on the other hand, is often seen as having 'won' — if only they had more time! They 'couldn't quite get there' but 'almost pinched the win' and have 'run into form'.

This is all to do with momentum and the trajectory of results. When your team is ahead and starts losing their lead, you are likely to remember the game for the sense of dread you had to endure. There's a pall over the performance. When your team comes from behind and is closing in on victory, there is a greater sense of optimism.

Boiled down, a win isn't always a win, and a loss isn't always a loss.

In business, this means we need to pay attention to the direction and timing of our 'wins', and how we communicate them. Overperforming in the first quarter can make results for the rest of the year more difficult psychologically to maintain. Coming home with the proverbial 'wet sail' will instead make us feel like champions!

For example:

A publicly listed company announces favourable results in the first half, but more moderate results in the back half of the year. Analysts and commentators start questioning their leadership, and morale within the company starts to flatten. Shareholders start selling, and staff start job hunting.

Another company structures its activities to secure modest first half results while accelerating growth in the second. Headlines celebrate their turnaround, bonuses get paid, and everyone looks forward to another successful year. The buzz attracts high calibre talent and investment.

See also:

-> Fuzzy Future Self, page 96
-> Zero-Sum is Dumb, page 162

39. Zero-Sum is Dumb

How to ask for a fair share

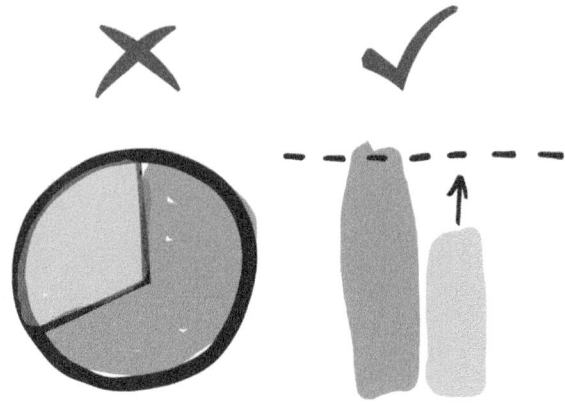

This is about:

Influencing people to give you more of something they have.

Which is important because:

People don't like to lose what they have, so if they see their share being eroded, they will be less willing to oblige.

We see this in the fight for equal rights. When positioned as gains for one group (e.g., women) coming at the expense of another (e.g., men), those in power who stand to lose will rail against it.

It works like this:

A Zero-Sum game is when one person's gain is another person's loss. The gain and loss balance out to zero.

Too often, when seeking additional resources, power or rights, the argument is framed as if using a pie chart. There's a finite amount of resources to be shared. 'We want what you have', is the theme. The problem is those who 'have it' won't want to give it up.

Instead, the argument needs to be framed as a metaphorical bar chart — a non-zero-sum proposition. The attainment of rights for one group does not come at the expense of another. For example, increasing the number of jobs available to people with a disability without changing the number of jobs available to those without disability. The theme this time is 'we just want the same as you want'. This uses common ground and is harder to argue against.

This plays out on the work front, too. Stakeholders clash over resources, and customers might close their mind to your product if they think resources are already allocated in that domain.

For example:

The management team is discussing budget allocations. Rather than make a request for 'a fair share of the marketing dollars' (pie chart framing), you instead request 'an allocation in line with revenue expectations' (bar chart framing).

See also:

-> PES-imistic Paradigm, page 38
-> Reactance Model, page 150
-> Frame the Gain Vs. Loss is Boss, page 154

40. Rage-O-Meter

Why you should cease inflammatory language

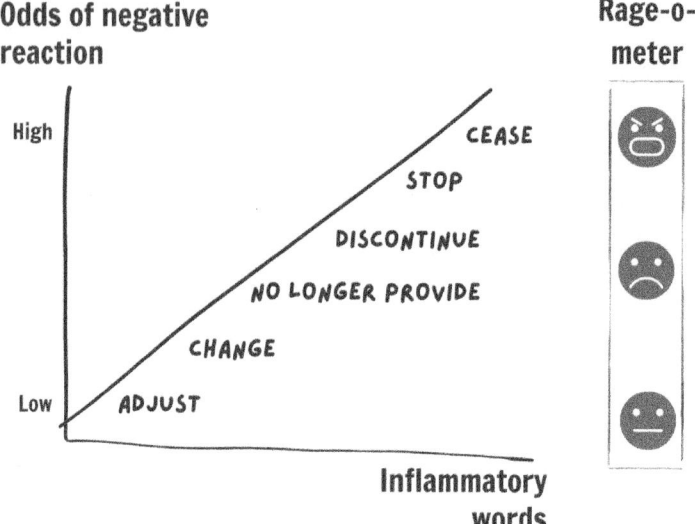

Odds of negative reaction

Rage-o-meter

High

CEASE
STOP
DISCONTINUE
NO LONGER PROVIDE
CHANGE

Low   ADJUST

Inflammatory words

This is about:

Reducing the odds people will react negatively to bad news.

Which is important because:

Bad news is a part of life, and you'll need to share it at some time or other. You want to do it in a way that is honest but also avoids inflaming the situation.

It works like this:

When people feel something is being taken away from them, it triggers 'loss aversion' and means they will respond negatively. Words that more strongly imply loss (like 'cease' or 'stop') are therefore more inflammatory.

For example:

Let's say you are changing a customer's service levels, which means they'll be getting less than they used to. Choose words to make the change acceptable rather than something that will make them angry. For example, 'we need to adjust your service levels' is more conciliatory than 'we will be ceasing your xyz service'.

See also:

-> PES-imistic Paradigm, page 38
-> Effective Emails, page 146
-> Frame the Gain Vs. Loss is Boss, page 154

41. Forget the Shit Sandwich

How to give verbal feedback

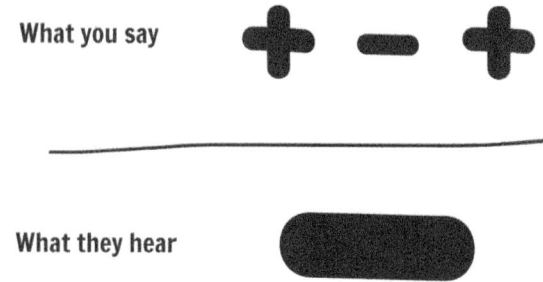

What you say

What they hear

This is about:

How to deliver negative feedback so that it's heard, understood and acted upon.

Which is important because:

Negative feedback is core to human relationships.

It works like this:

A popular approach to giving bad news, particularly in performance reviews, is to sandwich negative feedback between more positive information, a.k.a. the 'shit sandwich'.

'I really liked how you ran that last project but I think you need to work harder on your presentation skills. All in all, I think you are a great team player.'

It's a popular approach because it makes YOU feel better as the one sharing the criticism. You start on a positive and end on a positive, avoiding any social awkwardness.

There are two problems with this. First, most people are waiting for the 'but', missing any of the good news you want them to hear. This is largely due to 'negativity bias', which means we are wired to pay attention to the negative more than the positive.

Secondly, you are confusing the message, diluting the importance of something you see as an opportunity for them to work on.

Instead, demarcate the negative and positive and start your conversation by being clear about the structure you'll follow. This helps them know what to expect.

For example:

'Thanks for meeting with me. Today I want to cover off two aspects of your performance, as I see it. First, we'll cover areas I'd like to see some improvement, and second we'll talk through where you are excelling. Sound good?'

See also:

-> PES-imistic Paradigm, page 38
-> Empathy Map, page 108
-> Reactance Model, page 150

42. Certainty Matrix

What makes people ready to take risks

This is about:

How certainty about an outcome, and whether that outcome is good or bad, changes behaviour.

Which is important because:

You can influence a customer's perceptions of certainty, and therefore how likely they are to proceed.

It works like this:

There's an interplay between two dimensions — the degree of an outcome's **certainty** and whether that outcome is likely to be **positive or negative**.

Certain outcome

When an outcome is certain, your customer will act differently depending on whether the outcome is likely to be positive or negative.

1.   If the outcome is certain to be **positive**, they will be highly motivated to proceed and not want to miss out.

2.   If the outcome is certain to be **negative**, they will be looking for ways to avoid or minimise it, making them more open to take risks.

Uncertain outcome

Their behaviour changes too, when they are not sure what the outcome will be.

3.   If there's a chance the outcome will be **negative** but the situation is uncertain, they will likely be looking for ways to protect themselves from the bad thing happening.

4.   If there's more of a chance the outcome will be **positive**, they will likely proceed as long as it's not too much effort.

For example:

1.   **Certain positive outcome** – 'I want to lock this in'

Your customer chooses to buy floor tiles from you even though you're not the cheapest option because you can guarantee supply when they need it; a tradesperson who turns up on time gets lots of referrals as a result of their reputation for reliability; an airline famous for its safety record can charge more for flights.

2.   **Certain negative** – 'I may as well try'

Your customer comes to you because no one else can solve their problem; a patient opts for experimental treatment because they've been given a bad prognosis; an employee resigns before being fired.

3.   **Uncertain negative** – 'This would be good to have for peace of mind'

Your customer buys insurance because they want to reduce the risk of something bad happening — they don't want to worry about it; deciding to put money into cash-on-call bank account rather than superannuation so they can draw on it at any moment; upgrading your smartphone so you are less likely to run out of battery.

4.   **Uncertain positive** – 'Sure, it would be nice to have'

Your customer has a low care factor either way, but an 'in it to win it' philosophy gets them over the line; website visitors are willing to sign-up to your newsletter because it's easy enough to join for the 10% discount.

See also:

-> PES-imistic Paradigm, page 38
-> Frame the Gain Vs. Loss is Boss, page 154

PART 5.

MODELS FOR IMPROVING PERSONAL EFFECTIVENESS

Using ancient wiring to manage modern times

43. Murky Middle Model

How to prioritise Eisenhower's grey-area tasks

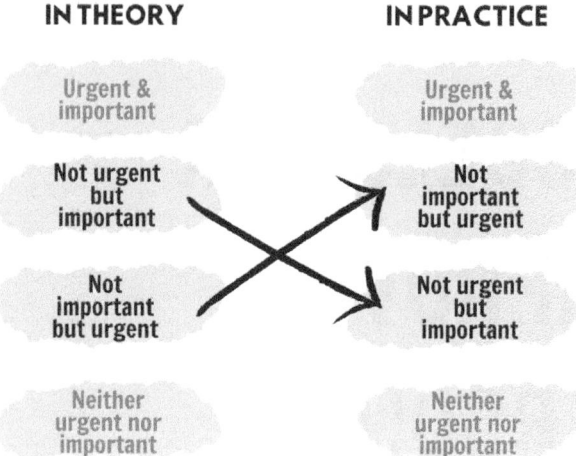

IN THEORY

Urgent &
important

Not urgent
but
important

Not
important
but urgent

Neither
urgent nor
important

IN PRACTICE

Urgent &
important

Not
important
but urgent

Not urgent
but
important

Neither
urgent nor
important

This is about:

Prioritising your time, the challenge of which lies in the murky middle of the Eisenhower Matrix*.

Which is important because:

Undertaking a task is often the easy thing. Deciding which tasks to do, in which order, is what can waste time and energy.

---

*The Eisenhower Matrix is a tool which helps designate tasks according to their urgency and importance.

You probably know to focus on important and urgent tasks, and to ignore tasks that are neither. The struggle is working out what to do with those that fall in the grey area — they might be not urgent but important, or important but not urgent.

It works like this:

The Eisenhower Matrix suggests placing important, non-urgent tasks ahead of those that are urgent but unimportant. This is fine in theory, and works when we are being cool-headed, rational decision-makers.

But in practice we focus more on the (illusion) of urgency than task importance. This is known as the 'Mere Urgency Effect'.

There are two realities about decision making:

1.   People are wired to be more concerned with what they stand to **lose than gain** (i.e., they are 'scared'), and this includes scarcity of time. Urgency, in other words, dominates our thinking.

2.   People respond to the needs of **Now Me** not Future Me (see Fuzzy Future Self, page 96). Now Me wants to get the urgent and obvious task done, leaving Future Me to tackle whatever is important...eventually.

While in theory you should prioritise important over urgent, in practice urgent probably gets your attention. If you want to change this, you'll need to employ some behavioural strategies.

For example:

Let's say you have an important presentation coming up next month. You also have an inbox full of emails. You know you should work on the presentation, but you promise yourself you'll do it once you've cleared your inbox.

Techniques to try:

· Focus on **outcomes** not timelines. This is known as 'outcome salience' and will help you prioritise the bigger picture. The outcome of your presentation, for example, will be more important in your performance review than your dedication to emails.

· Stop thinking of yourself as 'busy' because this is a time-related construct that feeds the urgency narrative. Instead think of yourself as '**productive**', which is more outcome related.

· Chunk the presentation task down into **smaller bites** so it feels less daunting. When daunted, we are more prone to seek distraction. Smaller morsels also mean you feel that you are accomplishing more, giving you the dopamine hit that you've been using emails for.

· **Disconnect** yourself from perceived urgency. Remind yourself that these 'urgent' tasks can wait. I've heard inboxes described as 'someone else's to-do list for you', and that can be a helpful way to refocus on what *you* want to get done.

· **Don't open** your emails until you have done at least an hour on your presentation.

· **Set boundaries.** Use an 'out of office' message on your emails to let people know to call you if the issue is actually urgent.

See also:

-> PES-imistic Paradigm, page 38
-> Fuzzy Future Self, page 96

44. The Multitasking Illusion

Leaking time through task switching

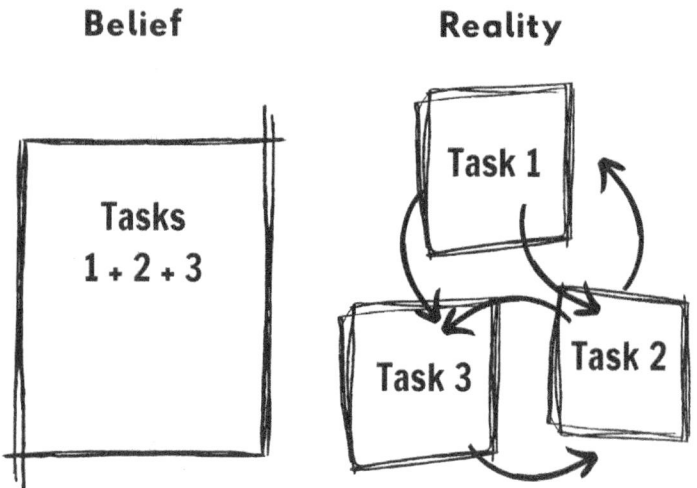

Belief   **Reality**

Tasks
1 + 2 + 3

Task 1

Task 3   Task 2

This is about:

Thinking we can multitask.

Which is important because:

People think they are being productive when undertaking multiple tasks at once, but they are actually undermining their effectiveness.

It depends, of course, on the types of tasks. Here we're talking about tasks that require cognitive effort and attention. You can multitask when you listen to a podcast while washing dishes, but not while reading a book.

It works like this:

What feels like multitasking is really task switching. We don't do this AND that. We do *this* THEN *that* THEN *this* and back to *that*.

In short, it's OR not AND, and when we switch tasks, we waste time and momentum. Estimates suggest trying to multitask costs as much as 40% of productive time — that's around three hours a day.

For example:

Your colleague is scrolling through emails while sitting in the team meeting. When challenged, they swear they can do both. The reality is they will be attuned to either what's being said *or* what they are reading, not both. The speed with which their brain switches between visual and auditory input gives them the impression they are attending to both, but that's not the case. For that reason, establishing team agreements about leaving phones out of reach can be a sensible move.

See also:

-> Forget the Shit Sandwich, page 166
-> Murky Middle Model, page 174

45. About Time

Why an hour feels shorter than that

60 minutes feels like...

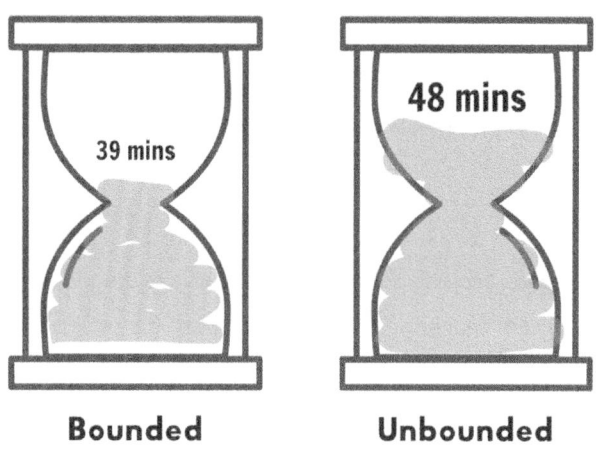

Bounded   **Unbounded**

This is about:

How we perceive time and why an hour often feels shorter than that.

Which is important because:

How we schedule our commitments can impact how well we use our time.

It works like this:

When you have a commitment pending, say a meeting at 2pm in the afternoon, you will tend to feel you have less 'free' time leading up to it. The pending commitment casts a shadow over you.

When your time is '**bounded**' because it butts up against a commitment, you are likely to perceive you have less time to accomplish tasks than when it is '**unbounded**' (obligation free). Research participants in a bounded condition, for example, felt they only had 39 minutes out of an hour to do what they wanted to do. In an unbounded condition, they felt they had a full 48 minutes.

Objectively, we know a bounded and unbounded hour are the same, but subjectively they feel different. As a result, whenever your time is bounded, you will be more likely to avoid longer tasks even when they are feasible to complete and undertake fewer shorter tasks than you would have if you were unbounded.

For example:

One night you are free from 7pm but have a friend coming over at 8pm. Another night you are free from 7pm but have no plans. In both cases you have an hour (at least) available. In the first case your time is 'bounded' because you have a commitment following, and in the second, it is 'unbounded' because your time is not limited. In the bounded case you are likely to read less of your book or watch less of your favourite TV program.

Let's look at your work week. On Monday you have meetings at 9am, 2pm and 4pm and can't seem to focus on anything between these commitments. You are distracted by what's coming up and find yourself constantly checking the clock. On Tuesday you have back-to-back meetings at 9am, 10am and 11am and because you've batched your commitments, find you can better focus throughout your day.

See also:

-> Murky Middle Model, page 174
-> The Multitasking Illusion, page 178

46. Peat Principle

How technology is changing how we think

Topsoil

Peat

This is about:

How we engage in learning and with information.

Which is important because:

Increasingly it feels like keeping up with, and retaining, what we should know is impossible — like we are drinking from a firehose.

It works like this:

Pre-Internet, knowledge was like peat. Dense and rich, taking time to develop through study, books and discourse.

Now knowledge is like topsoil. Easily washed away and expedient, and in many ways, superficial. Nothing seems to 'stick' like it used to.

It's not your imagination — it's your brain. The problem is that when we use search engines and social media, we don't lay neural pathways in our brains that help encode information. By outsourcing our thinking so we can keep up, we're getting sugar hits without nourishment.

To interrupt this pattern requires time away from the Internet. Time away from access to answers at your fingertips. Time away from rabbit holes and curiosities. More analogue experiences, fewer digital ones.

For example:

Time offline and distraction-free is sometimes referred to as 'focus work' or 'deep work'. The key is to remove yourself from your usual settings. You can do this physically, like going for a walk or sitting in a different place, and/or psychologically, by shifting your mindset. Dedicate time in the diary to this practice — make it a ritual so you look forward to it and can withstand the discomfort that may arise from not being distracted. And if you want to *really* embed new knowledge, teach it to someone else.

See also:

-> Trio of Truths About Your Customer, page 86
-> Meta Model for Influencing Action, page 196

47. Moderators Vs. Eliminators

How to modify habits

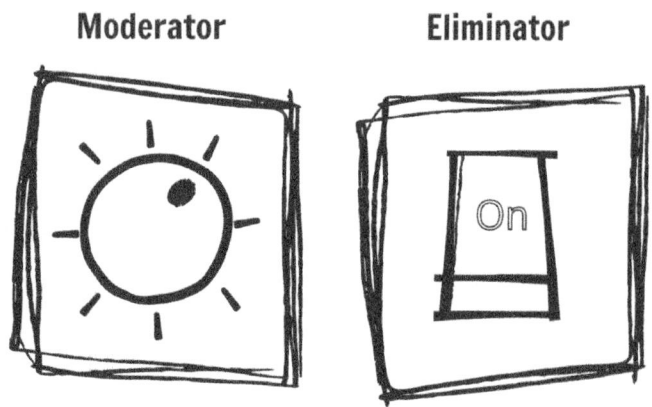

Moderator   **Eliminator**

This is about:

Finding an approach to changing habits that works for you.

Which is important because:

Different strategies work for different people, at different times.

It works like this:

Some people tend to be '**Eliminators**' — they best modify their behaviour by either allowing or eliminating it. It's a binary yes or no, in or out. Like an on/off light switch, chocolate is allowed in the house or it's not.

Others tend to be '**Moderators**' who best modify their behaviour b.
tempering it, more like a dimmer switch. Having a small amount of
something, like a square of chocolate, staves off the temptation to
binge the whole block.

The situation you are in, or the type of vice you have, may alter your
preferred approach. You might be an Eliminator in some contexts,
but Moderator in others, for example. When seeking to change
behaviour, experiment to see which approach works best for you.

	Moderator approach	Eliminator approach
Calories from food	Eat only until full	Fast on particular days
Alcohol	One glass per night	Not on weeknights
Smoking	Limit of two per day	Only allowed at social events
TV consumption	Only watch certain programs or during certain hours	Pull out plug, discard TV unit, eliminate during week
Social media	Limit time allowed	Remove Apps from phone
Work	Take on fewer tasks, space out workload	Work longer some days, not at all on others

See also:

-> Williams Behaviour Change Model, page 8
-> Partitioning Principle, page 66
-> Me-TT Model, page 104
-> Three C's of Habit Ease, page 188

's of Habit Ease

How to embed a new habit

Consistency

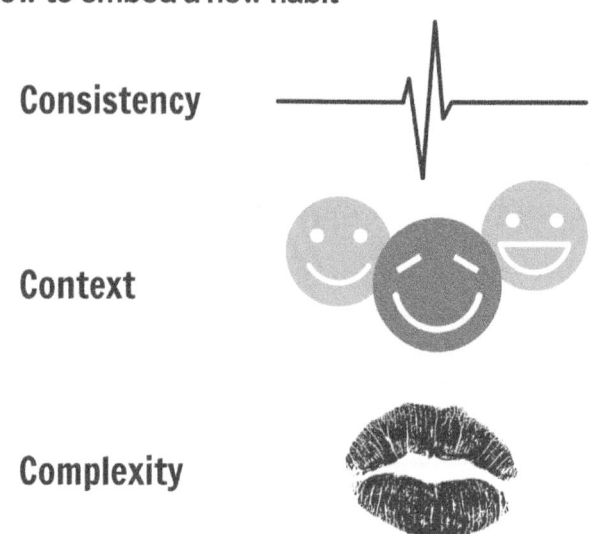

Context

Complexity

This is about:

How to support new habits.

Which is important because:

Habits are the keystone for a happy and productive life but it can be difficult to embed new behaviours.

It works like this:

There are three elements to pay attention to in order to give yourself the best chance of a new behaviour sticking.

Consistency

When adopting a new behaviour, the most important thing is turning up on a consistent basis. In this case, getting to the starting line is much more important than finishing. Go to the pool even if you swim only one lap. Roll out your yoga mat even if you don't complete a Vinyasa session. Pull out the chopping board even if you don't cook a meal.

By turning up consistently you are building a habit for the habit — a foundation of muscle memory that makes it easier to take the next step, and the one after that. Even if you have a minor disruption, consistency makes it easy to get back in the groove.

Context

The context in which the behaviour occurs is also key. That means setting up the physical environment to support the new behaviour, like putting your gym bag by the door so it's easy to grab on your way to work and making sure your social environment is supportive too, by spending time with people who already model the behaviour you are trying to adopt and distancing yourself from naysayers.

Complexity

Keeping things simple, stupid (K.I.S.S.) is essential to new habit success. While your plans to run a marathon or overhaul your diet may be grand, they can also be daunting and demotivating. Avoid anything that requires a lot of expensive and complicated new equipment, or that demands significant brain power. Plan for the days when you have zero energy or enthusiasm because being able to continue at your lowest ebb will give you the greatest chance of success.

For example:

Let's say you are trying to build a habit of making home-cooked meals rather than ordering take away.

· **Consistency** – You decide that you will cook on Mondays–Thursdays at home. The first week you still order takeaway but make sure you put the chopping board on the bench. This becomes a visual reminder of the intent to cook.

· **Context** – You get your partner's buy-in by telling them it's something that is important to you and create a playlist to cook to so that you enjoy the time in the kitchen.

· **Complexity** – You decide to use a meal-kit service that delivers a recipe and ingredients, eliminating the need for you to think about what to cook and go shopping.

See also:

-> Trio of Truths About Your Customer, page 86
-> Hot-Cold Empathy Gap, page 92
-> Moderators Vs. Eliminators, page 186

49. Creation Vs. Curation

How value is shifting from creation to curation

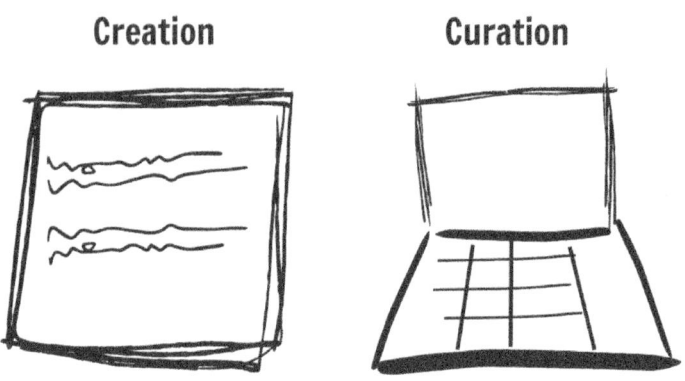

Creation   **Curation**

This is about:

Time and attention poor customers may value curation of ideas more than creation.

Which is important because:

Creation used to be where the effort (and value) lay. Now it's about curation.

It works like this:

In the past, writers would draft in longform. Then, to have work published, they'd have to transcribe their handwritten notes by typewriter.

Not only did it save them money to have fewer words to print, but it also saved a lot of typing, too.

Writers would therefore edit ruthlessly to avoid effort that didn't add value. Pieces that started with 6,000 words were pared back to 3,000.

These days not only are most works published online where the first word costs the same as the last, writers type as they go. The act of writing is the act of typing. Each word is a sunk cost of the creative process. Instead of being motivated to cull words, writers are motivated to keep them, sidestepping the unpleasantness of 'killing their darlings'. Bloated articles that start with 9,000 words stay at 9,000 words.

There are two broader points to be made.

First, people will expend a little effort to save a lot of effort, as writers used to do. They will not expend effort if the benefits for doing so are unclear, though, as is the case with modern writers. Where effort used to be in service of the creative reward, and therefore palatable, now it stands as its own burden to be avoided. What we create suffers as a result.

When managing a business, the question is what constraints should you impose to get a higher quality outcome? Are you rewarding the right kind of effort?

Second, value has shifted from creation — the crafting the work — to curation, the ability to pare back or synthesise the work. Customers want less to do, not more.

For example:

When developing a product, more is not necessarily better. There's a discipline in curating the experience for your customer. Apple does this well, ensuring their products work straight out of the box.

See also:

-> Effort Vs. Reward Equation, page 28
-> The Porter Principle, page 32
-> PES-imistic Paradigm, page 38
-> Partitioning Principle, page 66

50. Meta Model for Influencing Action

Why you are central to influencing action

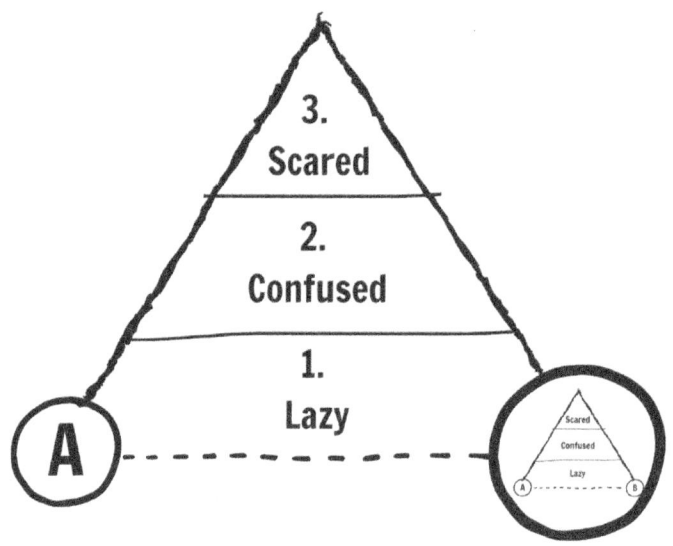

This is about:

The final and most important lesson when it comes to influencing action: to change what others do you first need to change what you do.

Which is important because:

We often identify tools and techniques to use on others, forgetting that using these new tools requires us to adopt new behaviours.

It works like this:

Not only is the person (or people) you are seeking to influence lazy, scared and confused (page 8), you are too!

That means you will get stuck in your existing status quo (A. Not using behavioural techniques) unless you influence yourself to move to the new status quo (B. Using behavioural techniques).

For example:

Your behavioural objective (A to B) is to use behavioural techniques to influence others to take action.

To get yourself to adopt this new behaviour, identify and address the three barriers to your own action.

1.   **Lazy** – How can you make it easy and rewarding to bother?

2.   **Confused** – How can you clarify what you want to do so you don't get overwhelmed? What can you default to? What's the one thing you will try this week?

3.   **Scared** – What's the worst that can happen if you try and it doesn't succeed? How can you nullify that scenario? What can you make yourself fear about NOT trying?

See also:

-> Williams Behaviour Change Model, page 8
-> Williams Behaviour Change Venn, page 20

51. Mega Model

An overview of models in The Williams Behaviour Book

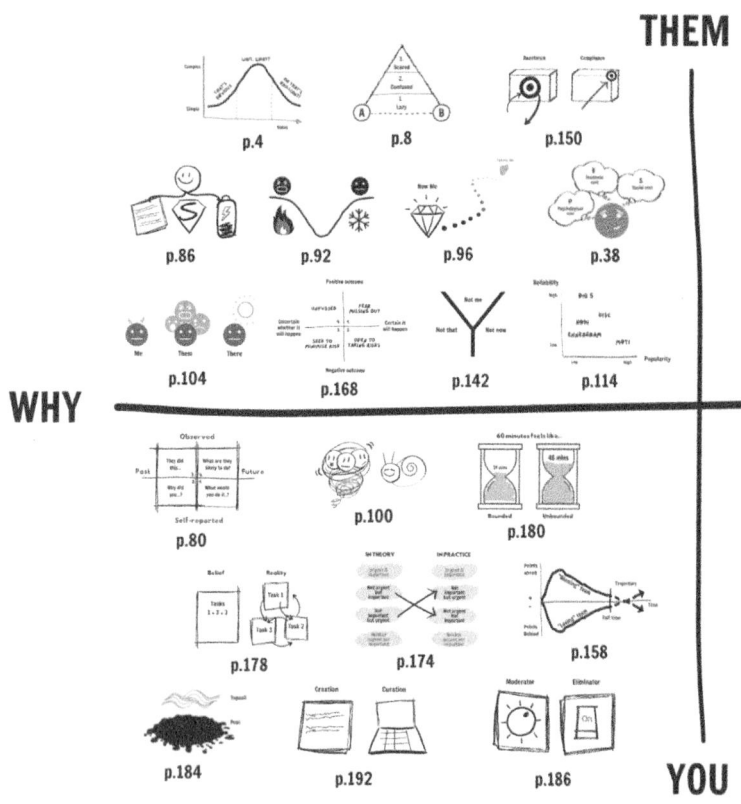

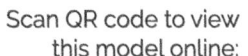

Scan QR code to view
this model online:

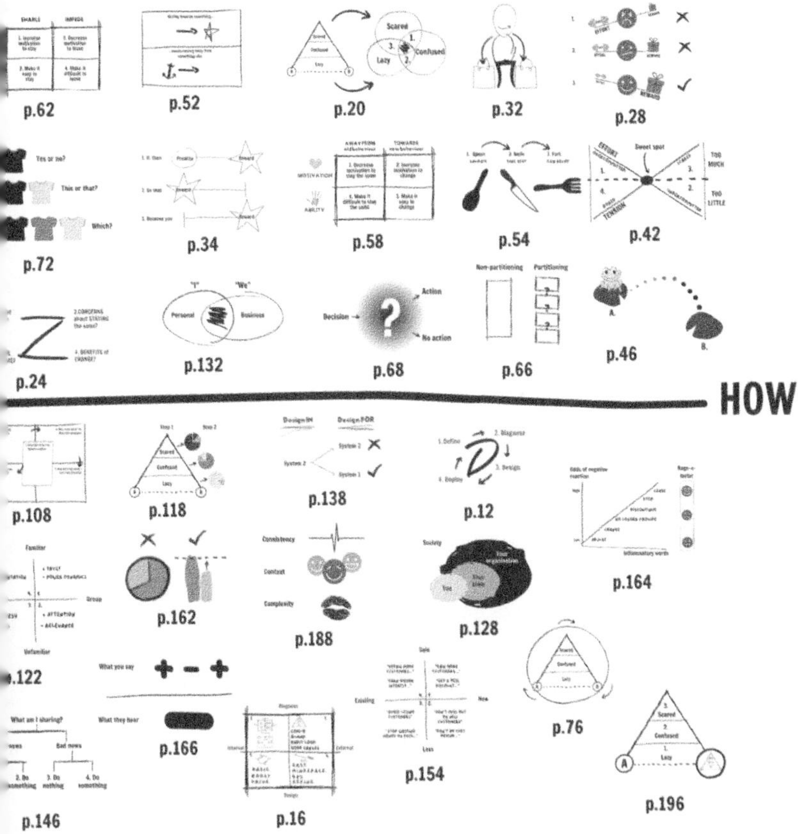

p.62

p.52

p.20

p.32

p.28

p.72

p.34

p.58

p.54

p.42

p.24

p.132

p.68

p.66

p.46

HOW

p.108

p.118

p.138

p.12

p.164

p.122

p.162

p.188

p.128

p.146

p.166

p.16

p.154

p.76

p.196

Why they...

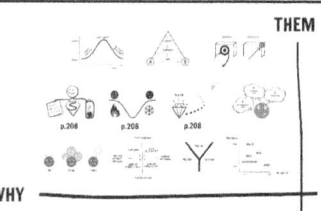

How to make them...

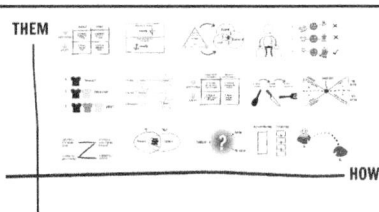

How to make them...	Model (and model number)	Page #
Engage with you	Behavioural Bowtie (11)	42
Buy	Conversational Cutlery (14)	54
Leave their status quo	Lily Pad Leaping Lesson (12)	46
Move forward by letting go	Move Away Vs. Move Towards (13)	52
Bother to proceed	Effort Vs. Reward Equation (7)	28
Want to work with you	The Porter Principle (8)	32
Stay	Customer Retention Strategies (16)	62
Stop	Partitioning Principle (17)	66
Choose	Choosing Choices (19)	72
Follow through	Decision-Action Conversion (18)	68
Want to change	Zorro Technique (6)	24
Change	Williams Behaviour Change Venn (5)	20
Do what you want	Williams Change Quadrant (15)	58
Motivated to work	Timing Rewards (9)	34
Advocate for you	Arming Your Advocate (32)	132

Why you...

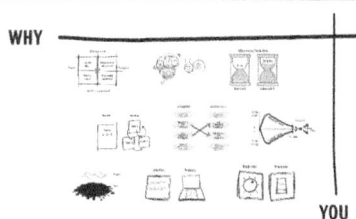

How to make yourself...

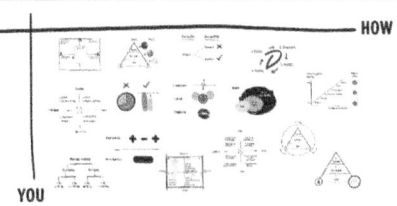

YOU — HOW

How to make yourself...	Model (and model number)	Page #
See things from a different point of view	Empathy Map (27)	108
Scale across segments	BE-gmentation (29)	118
Design for your audience	Designing Mindset (33)	138
Adapt to your audience	Influencing Individuals Vs. Groups (30)	122
Communicate more effectively	Frame the Gain Vs. Loss is Boss (37)	154
Avoid turning them off	Rage-O-Meter (40)	164
Write better emails	Effective Emails (35)	146
Heard when giving feedback	Forget the Shit Sandwich (41)	166
Ask for more	Zero-Sum is Dumb (39)	162
Apply what you've learnt	Meta Model for Influencing Action (50)	196

How to make yourself (continued)...

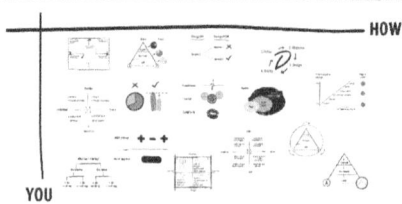

How to make yourself...	Model (and model number)	Page #
Come up with solutions	D-Process for Developing Behavioural Solutions (3)	12
Identify influencing opportunities	360 Degree BE (31)	128
Choose the right behavioural model	Behavioural Models Overview (4)	16
Change your habits	Three C's of Habit Ease (48)	188
Sustain behaviour change	The Williams Wheel (20)	76

Alphabetical Index of Models

P

R

S

T

W

Y

Z

Acknowledgements

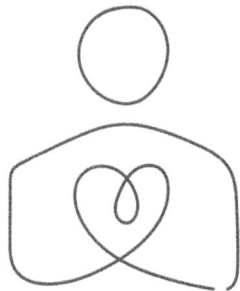

When we share our stories of life, we tend to do so with the benefit of hindsight, stepping on only the most obvious stones. In writing this book, I am similarly struck by how easy the dots seemed to join. How can it be that they weren't joined before?

The truth – in life and in writing a book – is that the experience is meandering. There are unproductive side alleys, missteps and frustrations.

It is with great joy, therefore, to acknowledge those who helped me bring this book to you. Some directly, with editorial input and content advice, and others indirectly, by caring about me and my work.

I'll start by thanking Lynne Cazaly. Unbeknownst to me at the time, the seeds of this book were planted when I interviewed Lynne for my Talking Talks series, during which we discussed how important visuals are to clarify ideas and galvanise workplaces.

And what could be better than drawing on behavioural science?

Speaking of which, this book can only exist because of 'The Science' made and shared by hard working researchers and academics. While I decided not to reference individual studies in this book, my enduring thanks to those at the forefront of understanding why we do what we do.

To those with whom I entrusted a rough and ready draft, thank you for your thoughtful and thought-provoking feedback. Particular thanks to Sam Tatam, Suzanne Tonks, Jon Manning, Keith Williams and Daniel Ross for zeroing in on exactly those aspects of the book that were troubling me and providing helpful suggestions.

To my grammar conscience Catherine King and editor Leyla Fitzpatrick, you've performed the ultimate expert glow-up. The draft mooched into your inboxes in trackie dacks and ugg boots, and sashayed back, runway ready. Thank you!

To my community of neighbours who got me through our perpetual lockdowns, especially Sues and Danielle Tonks, and Rachael and Chris Bourke, your friendship and support is a large part of why I love living where we do.

To my inner sanctum of friends, Catherine King, Sonya Constantine Dowe, Renee Koliba and Maree Whiting, it's the chats we have that fill my cup. Sometimes with tea, often with wine and always with love.

Finally to my family. Keith and Jenny, Luke, Natalie, Ava and Ella, Milli and Lexi, I love you all.

The Williams
Behaviour Book Resources

To get free access to additional resources:

· Visit https://www.briwilliams.com/WBBR, or

· Scan the QR code below

Use your unique code, printed on the Copyright page at the beginning of this book, to download each model's png file for free.

About the author

Bri Williams is one of Australia's leading authorities on behavioural influence.

A CPA with a degree in Applied Psychology, Bri founded People Patterns in 2011, a specialist consultancy that helps businesses get staff, customers and stakeholders to take action. Prior to this she worked in finance, HR and product management for some of Australia's leading brands.

A regular contributor to Smartcompany and host of Talking Talks, Bri has written multiple books, including "Behavioural Economics for Business" and "The How of Habits", and appears regularly as a presenter, panellist and media commentator.

Bri lives in Melbourne and works with clients across Australia and around the world. More information can be found at www.briwilliams.com

How to get in touch

Follow Bri on Twitter and Instagram @peoplepatterns

Watch Bri on www.youtube.com/@BriWilliams

Email Bri via bri@peoplepatterns.com.au

Connect with Bri on LinkedIn

Call Bri on +61 408 392 173